Using Pop Culture to Teach Information Literacy

Using Pop Culture to Teach Information Literacy

Methods to Engage a New Generation

Linda D. Behen

LIBRARIES

UNLIMITED

A Member of the Greenwood Publishing Group

Westport, Connecticut • London

Library of Congress Cataloging-in-Publication Data

Behen, Linda D.
    Using pop culture to teach information literacy : methods to engage a
new generation / by Linda D. Behen.
        p. cm.
    Includes bibliographical references and index.
    ISBN 1-59158-301-2 (pbk : alk. paper)
    1. Information literacy—Study and teaching (Secondary)—United States.
2. Library orientation for high school students—United States. 3. High
school libraries—Activity programs—United States. 4. Popular
culture—Study and teaching (Secondary)—United States. I. Title.
ZA3075.B43   2006
028.7071′273—dc22   2006003710

British Library Cataloguing in Publication Data is available.

Library of Congress Catalog Card Number: 2006003710
ISBN: 1-59158-301-2

First published in 2006

Libraries Unlimited, 88 Post Road West, Westport, CT 06881
A Member of the Greenwood Publishing Group, Inc.
www.lu.com

Printed in the United States of America

∞™

The paper used in this book complies with the
Permanent Paper Standard issued by the National
Information Standards Organization (Z39.48–1984).

10 9 8 7 6 5 4 3 2

Contents

Acknowledgments

To Frances Romweber, principal of Saint Ursula Academy, whose constant support, encouragement, and trust over the last eight years has allowed me to experiment and grow as an educator.

To all my colleagues, friends, and students at St. Ursula Academy with whom I've shared laughs, tears, struggles, and accomplishments. Work shouldn't be this much fun!

To my family and friends who have always believed in me.

Thank You

Introduction

What a great time to be a school librarian! We have at our fingertips efficient research methods and resources along with communication toys that quickly become educational tools.

My day is never the same as the one before, and I prefer it that way. I am easily bored. And in my effort to keep my students and me awake and interested during the course of the day and school year, I constantly look for new and improved ways to do things. I love taking the mundane and recreating it into something sparkly and bright that will engage students. That's my motivation and excuse for exploring, adapting, playing, and integrating popular culture into my library instruction.

Talking is required in my library and I constantly challenge students to question and suggest better ways to do things. I encourage freedom of thought and diverse methods of learning. I keep my library program changing and growing, and I'm not afraid to admit failure. I've stood in front of students (more than once) who could barely keep their eyes open and continued to blah, blah, blah my library orientation and information literacy tips despite their apathy and my own boredom. I've played the *Survivor* or *The Amazing Race* game with students up to the last bell on Friday before a school break and barely survived it myself. I do learn from my mistakes and seem constantly to make new ones. Yet despite my occasional errors or miscalculations, I do keep trying to connect with my students and to help them develop into information-literate young adults.

I have been blessed with a supportive environment that encourages growth and experimentation. As a result, I've seen some successes in the past few years. I've had graduates return to visit who tell me that they are so much better prepared for college research than their classmates are. Our circulation statistics for fiction and non–curriculum-related reading materials has doubled over the last few years, and we always have a few students who hang out during lunch wanting to talk about books. I actually see students choosing proprietary databases over Internet search engines for both academic and personal information.

I know that most students are far too polite to tell me that they hate the instructional games we play when they come to the library, and I've wondered occasionally if I should approach information literacy instruction more seriously as a card-carrying library professional. Nonetheless, I continue using pop culture in my library program because the students' verbal and nonverbal feedback indicate that they enjoy the features we've added for their pleasure and learning. Students almost always ask to play the library game and to compete for our grand prizes as they enter the library with a class. Teachers assure me that they retain information better and that they see results through their students' projects and assignments. So who am I to take myself and my job so seriously? I'm giving them what they want and what they are comfortable with. They are part of a generation that understands technology, collaborative work, and pop culture. I am here to serve them and to educate them, and I choose to use the tools that interest them.

I challenge you to make your information literacy instruction come alive with the suggestions in the following chapters or to find that certain something that you and your students find interesting and fun. I plead with you to lighten up and not to take yourself and your job so seriously and to allow a little fun into your library. Watch how quickly students respond and enjoy using the pop culture themes.

A special thanks goes out to the students of St. Ursula Academy who have participated, enjoyed, and even encouraged my instructional methods. These young women are proving to be very prepared for a changing world, and I'm proud to be a part of their education and growth as lifelong learners.

Chapter 1

Today's Teens, Technology, and Pop Culture

WHO ARE THEY?

Are students today so different from those of previous generations? The media report a serious discussion about today's youth and their connection with technology. We see them at the malls with cell phones glued to their ears, at coffee shops tapping text messages on their phones, playing video games on computers and in arcades, blogging, e-mailing, or live chatting at home and at school. They shop online for movie tickets, clothes, ring tones, upgrades to their technology toys, and music.

The media often present the negative aspects of the relationship between kids and technology and warn the public about the dangers of chat rooms and too much time spent with TV and video games. Despite what the media tell us, there are many positive aspects of technology that must be acknowledged, permitted, and sometimes even encouraged by adults who interact with this generation.

In our schools, we no longer need to prepare for technology. It's here, our students are comfortable with it, and we need to keep up even when it pushes us beyond our comfort zone.

A few years ago, schools banned cell phones and e-mail. Today, most schools embrace both. It was not a case of giving in to the inevitable but of discovering the value. The newest complaints are that students don't correspond enough via e-mail with teachers or use their school e-mail accounts. We expect that they will use their cell phones to communicate with parents in times of unscheduled early dismissals or forgotten homework or lunches. And aren't we annoyed when students don't have a cell phone and want to borrow ours? Cell phones are now only banned when they interfere with others' rights; for example, students cannot use cell phones in classrooms or the library because others need a space free from distraction and others' conversations.

If this trend with today's youth is considered a revolution, it is almost opposite to the revolution of their parents and the baby boomers. These teens and young adults aren't crying anti-establishment rhetoric or protesting war; in our observations, they like their parents, rebel less outwardly, and are good at team and group work. In fact, they thrive on supporting and embracing others. Schools and students rely on peer mentor and buddy programs to help students adjust and succeed in high school, and tutoring and homework sessions are initiated by students for students. Co-leader positions are replacing the single presidency, chairs, and other student leadership positions in many schools so that collaboration and teamwork are stressed and utilized.

It's obvious that the students who come into our schools and school libraries are different from students just ten years ago, not only because they are team players and not necessarily in terms of material goods and money (although that seems obvious with all the teen consumption occurring at the local mall), but because they have, understand, and embrace technology. In addition, they have different relationships with their parents and adults than teens of generations past. Our students tell us how they consider their parents to be their friends and how they can talk with them about almost anything.

What can we make of this, and how does it affect us in our school libraries? Today's students do not need or want us to make their lives at school simple and carefree without academic rigor. They do need and wish us to accept them as unique individuals. Our students' trusting relationships with their parents may open the door for us as educators to have better relationships with them. If we can build on the comfortable interaction that they have with their parents, we should be able to approach their different literacy and media needs and interests as a partnership. We can use what they are already comfortable with to make their academic pursuits more efficient and successful. As educators, it is our responsibility to teach them what is relevant to their lives and to do so in ways that they find meaningful.

If the popular culture of today's teens is what drives their behavior and motivates them, why not use it to connect with them?

CAN WE BLAME IT ON POP CULTURE?

Throughout history, adults have worried about teens and their connection to popular culture. Dime novels, comic books, jazz music, tight jeans and ducktails, rock-and-roll, movies, dirty dancing, and video games have been blamed for creating rebellious and violent teens. Each day, in newspapers and on talk shows, experts in child development and psychology blame television and the media for putting dangerous ideas into our youths' heads. Yet literature of centuries past, including Shakespeare, Dickens, and Austen, warns against the rambunctious nature of youth and youthful fashion, and their literary characters frequently face bleak situations as a result of impulsive and impatient traits as the ultimate warning against misbehavior. It is interesting that things haven't really changed much throughout history.

Is life in today's world more dangerous and so different as the media leads us to believe? Reports of teen shootings at Columbine High School in Colorado and weekend drinking binges at parties and on college campuses make us fearful that our youth are more at risk than ever. Is it appropriate to blame popular culture for this negative behavior and its results that we see daily in the media? Pop culture is a single factor among many that influence behavior. Other factors may include poverty, the high rate of divorce, and pressure from parents, school, peers, and teens themselves to succeed. It's obvious that those pressures and influences affect each individual differently. One cannot forget, however, the many positive influences and the support that youth receive from their families, schools, television and movies, churches, and other sources.

Youth's fashion and communication styles, music, and interests often baffle adults, but don't we, as educators, family, friends, and parents of these teens, enjoy observing the differences among generations? Many of their interests catch on with older generations; teens aren't the only ones enjoying many of the popular fads, reality TV shows, and fashions that exist today. Multiple earrings were a youthful trend a decade or two ago, but have you noticed how many middle-aged and older women now have a row of earrings marching up their lobes? Discussion in our faculty lunchroom provides evidence that most of our teachers and staff members enjoy the same movies, television shows, and music that our students enjoy. Even if you've taken a vow to boycott reality television and not to acknowledge rap as music, shouldn't educators know as much as possible about what interests our adolescents so that we can do our job with them to the best of our ability? What else but pop culture gives us a snapshot image or definition of a specific time in our history and world? Who can't connect Rosie the Riveter, Elvis, hot rods, the Concord, and disco with a year, a decade, or an era?

Chapter 2

Why Does Library Instruction Need to Be Fun?

WHAT STUDENTS WANT

Students want instant gratification, and there are not enough hours in the day to teach them otherwise. Quite frankly, don't we find ourselves with expectations of instant gratification from our interaction and instruction with them? We'd love it if they absorbed and assimilated every tip, trick, and suggestion we offer. That's a great dream—but back to the real world. To do what we can with the time we have, we need to focus on the priorities of our library instruction program. The bottom line is that we need to put our students on the path to becoming information literate with information literacy skills that serve them well in college and beyond.

This book doesn't intend to answer the "whys" and "hows" of this young generation but is intended to be a practical approach to reaching teens in the library with methods that spark their curiosity and interest. We are school librarians who work hard every day to help our students become more information savvy, and it's obvious that students can be reached despite the difference in our ages, backgrounds, and cultures. At the very least, we should respect and admire their comfort with new technologies and know that they can teach us a lot about staying tuned in and aware of the changing world.

SETTING PRIORITIES FOR INSTRUCTION

How do we set priorities for our information literacy instruction? It isn't easy, and the only constant is that it's a dynamic process. We start at the beginning with our younger students, and we jump forward when we realize that they have mastered the basics. It's often necessary for us to go backward and review and bring everyone up to the same level of understanding. We constantly add and delete from our instruction and use newer and better technology and methods. As assignments change, we change. Our aim is to be intuitive so we can read students' needs and wants and adapt to them. Information literacy doesn't happen after one, two, or three instructional sessions in the library, no matter how wonderful the instruction.

Constant reinforcement by library staff and teachers in every year the student spends at a school is needed. It's so much easier when information literacy terms, expectations, and assessments are standardized and understood throughout the school with a schoolwide research model (see Chapter 5) so that students know for sure that their new teacher has the same expectations as their last teacher.

Our goal in information literacy and skills instruction is to prepare students for their current and future relationship with information. Our libraries and the information we gather are no longer limited to the walls in which they live and within which our students sit. Information seeking is now a global pursuit and almost limitless. Our immediate job is to identify the needs of our students and to offer an organized manner of locating the information that satisfies those needs.

It doesn't take a lot of intuition to know that, in general, students enter the library expecting to be bored. The shushing and possibly less than dynamic librarians and media specialists from past library experiences have formed their attitudes and expectations. We can change those attitudes. We are today's library goddesses and gods who understand what students want and need (at least we are willing to find out), and we will give them what they need in the ways that they find meaningful. It is essential that we don't miss opportunities to reach students and to give them the gift of information literacy.

Students only know the world as being information bloated. They have been presented with information bites and bits since they were babes, and they see a natural partnership with themselves and information. This confidence and comfort present some problems. Dangerously, students think they are information literate because they are technology literate and information aware. They do know how to find something about anything. But it's that "something" that isn't always credible, reliable, and appropriate for academic purposes—or any purpose. Sometimes they are unlucky, and their teachers don't recognize that the information used in an assignment isn't the best. Those experiences give positive reinforcement to their poor searching and information-gathering habits.

As Carol Tells's (1999, p. 4) article "Generation What? Connecting with Today's Youth" argues, "Too many adults have been either hostile or oblivious to teen cyberculture" and that hostility "extends into the classroom which creates a greater disconnect between how kids learn and communicate in their free time and how they are taught in school." The article goes so far as to blame adults who are reluctant to understand technology and its appeal to young people as causing kids to be abandoned by the system, which leads to irresponsible and dangerous situations.

WHAT STUDENTS NEED

Here are some practical reasons that demonstrate why we need to reach students where they live.

One Unsuccessful Research Session Breeds More Googling

When attempting new methods and slowing down to evaluate material results, students turn in frustration to what they know best and with what they are comfortable. Don't we all?

Is it a hopeless situation? Absolutely not. If students can learn how to download lyrics, bypass filtering systems, program a VCR or TIVO, and master an X-Box or Nintendo, they can learn to discern between worthy and useless information. By developing a research process, they will gain efficiency in finding those preferred sources that really satisfy their information needs and give them a basis for developing knowledge and wisdom. Students quickly develop an appreciation for the quality of proprietary databases, scholarly sources, and primary sources when they walk away with what they recognize as useful resources ready to be assimilated into their assignments.

Our students are the masters of multitasking and learning quickly. What seems to be difficult for them is knowing what is the right information for a specific purpose or when they have enough information. Some students leave the library only when they run out of time printing or e-mailing every title in the result list they've retrieved from their first and only keyword search. They don't read past the first paragraph or look for a key theme in the information to know if it satisfies their information need. For them, more is better. They'll deal with the specifics later. And we know what they do when they get home. They'll toss the "specifics" away without reading past the first few articles. They end up wasting much time and perhaps a lot of paper.

This problem results from not having a clue about how research relates to their class assignment or project. They know it's a required step because their teacher demands that they acquire a number of pieces of information, but what they don't understand is that information comes in many forms, styles, and qualities and that this information that they discover is the foundation of their learning and knowledge. Do they know the difference between a textbook or encyclopedic entry and an interview with an expert on black holes? Do they care if information about the Middle Ages comes from an article in *Time* magazine or from *Shakespeare Quarterly*? Do they have any clue as to why they should care?

It is our job to demonstrate to them why they should care. Ask them if they know who writes for *Newsweek* or the *New York Times* or what type of education is necessary to become a journalist and to land a job with one of those big magazines and newspapers. Then ask them about experts in a specific field. What education must they have, where do they work, what do they write, for whom, and in what journals and magazines does their work appear? After this discussion, enlightenment involving credibility, peer-reviewed material, and scholarly sources should be unfolding before them, and a new understanding will slowly brighten in their eyes.

How you fit information about primary sources, proprietary databases, publishing, copyright and plagiarism, and all the pieces of information literacy into your instruction is an individual decision as long as it gets covered somewhere. Luckily, many research models and standards are already available for us to use with our students. We don't need to create a brand new one to maintain a deliberate method of teaching information literacy.

Most information literacy models such as the Big6™ (Eisenberg, 2001–2005) or the Research Cycle (McKenzie, 2004) include steps that will satisfy the information literacy issues stated earlier, and school librarians can adapt and recreate a model for their own schools (see Chapter 8). The hardest step is the enforcement of the model in a consistent manner throughout the school so that every student in every class has the same learning opportunities and reinforcement will occur.

Even though we can remove the guesswork from the research puzzle and replace it with a step-by-step guide to solve any information need, we will see some resistance from students. This is why it's so important for us to incorporate themes and trends into the instruction to engage our students. Research unfolds more slowly and deliberately than students naturally like. They haven't the experience to know that something valuable is at the end of the long process of much trial and error. Students' involvement with the sometimes lengthy and painful steps during the information-seeking process is where critical thinking occurs and where learning and understanding takes place.

Good Research Skills Cut Down on Wasted Time

Time is precious for us—for teachers and for students who have more structured lives today than ever before. Homework and research are squeezed in between sport schedules, music lessons, shopping, and school clubs. Our teachers describe students who want it all; they want to be president of student council and of the service club, or they play two sports and have a job at the mall. We are competing with all the interests and needs in their lives, and it is imperative that we give them information in ways that are meaningful to them; otherwise, we will be dismissed, and the information won't be heard or remembered.

Be honest with students and tell them that your goal isn't to make them into instant librarians or to torture them with complicated steps of research. You'll see their expressions change and defensiveness drop when they are told that your goal is to save them time and make them more efficient researchers so that their priority is to assimilate useful information into their assignment so that they can learn, get a good grade, and move on with their lives. Before warning about the Internet and how it should be at the bottom of their list of possible resources to search, remind them that you use the Web every day—maybe a hundred times a day—but it's never the first place to look for information for an academic purpose. Explain how a Web site differs from a proprietary database that lives on the Internet, and offer examples of finding information for your teachers or principal that they've requested from you. Describe the process you've used to discover information for a presentation or for a teacher's class research project. Maybe it's the discovery that a principal or teacher has information needs the same as everyone else, but it works and is very effective in explaining why searching proprietary databases is a much better choice for locating important information (especially when your job or grade might depend on it).

To make scholarly material more appealing to students, make search engines less appealing. Require students to submit a Web site page evaluation form for each Internet page they use (see Chapter 7) for an assignment. Explain to them that the purpose of the form is to teach them how to evaluate and analyze Web sites and that for those who prefer not to take the time filling out the form, they can use reliable proprietary databases or your library catalog to locate Web sites and other information. Remind them over and over that it's more efficient for them to locate the credible information they need through the subscription databases and skip filling out the Web site evaluation form. At the end of the lesson, ask how filling out the Web site evaluation form can be avoided, and you'll see how well students can remember the steps to avoid extra work.

Sleeping Students Are Contagious

Students don't want to appear more interested than their friends, and they certainly don't want to seem dorky. Grab the attention of the kids who set the tone for the class. Just as these leaders can influence negatively, they can also influence in positive ways. The enthusiasm they exhibit will move around the room quickly.

Interactive instruction and student-centered learning allows students to teach each other. It keeps them thinking and engaged, and it's a natural for information literacy. As librarians, we move into the role of choreographer and allow students to do the teaching. Their curiosity, mistakes, successes, and energy are far more influential than anything we can say or do. But remember that students need and want structure—provide that and let it roll. For example, ask for a volunteer (or volunteer a student who you know can demonstrate successfully and has some influence in the class) to complete a library catalog search for a book about teens in the Middle East. Remind the student that we don't know whether a specific author would use the term *teen, teenager, child,* or *adolescent* to describe a certain age group and that since the Middle East consists of many individual countries as well as regions, an author might prefer to focus on a single region or an individual country. Finally, suggest that she search as specifically and efficiently in a single search strategy. Urge the class to help out and offer suggestions to the volunteer. Before you know it, the search will include truncation, Boolean elements, and a variety of searching techniques, and if it doesn't, you can continue to prompt for these. The students get credit for the result even though your reminders and questions urged them forward in the right direction. The class is now focused on the task, and students are actively teaching each other in a positive way.

It's not a natural fit for many of us to be choreographers and to be brave enough to allow the energy in the library to determine the path. The search example just given could have turned out badly if the librarian didn't help and direct the student(s) toward a solution and if the students hadn't been guided toward constructive suggestions. Planning and practice helps with your comfort and ability in allowing students to teach each other. Good instruction comes from a desire to have a connection with your students and from your effort to make it interesting to them. Ideas, suggestion, and styles can be taught, but the innate drive or need to help them discover a new understanding and knowledge cannot. As librarians, our time is more limited than classroom teachers. We can't play a video on the days after a bad night's sleep. If we don't seize the moment, it may not appear again. Good instruction develops from sturdy architecture. You want much of what happens in the session to be spontaneous and directed by the personalities and interaction of students in the class, but be confident knowing that it is structured by the solid walls of your instruction. Let yourself have a little fun with the students and let them know that you care as much about them as their information literacy skills. Some of the most teachable moments are born from students' and teachers' mistakes and the situations that arise from them.

Healthy Academic Competition Can Be Invigorating for Both Students and Librarians

Allow students to compete with each other and with you. Break the class into teams and let them work as groups. Challenging students to outsmart you is an obvious way to get your students to interact—what student doesn't want to prove how much smarter he or she is than an adult? Reward students for coming up with original ideas that you don't mention, original strategies for finding information, or a computer tip or shortcut. The reward and acknowledgment encourages more interaction and suggestions. Students appreciate humility from authority figures. Surprise your students and announce during your instruction that despite being a library goddess or god, you can't possibly know everything about information or remember all the important things day to day. Challenge them to offer additional tips and suggestions. If you're playing a game, offer bonus points for those with original responses. Isn't it much better to be humbled with successful students than to be the smartest in the room with unsuccessful students?

Games and competitions for library instruction are fun for everyone. When shortened class time cuts instruction time, it's tempting to skip the game, under the assumption that older students might prefer a quicker, unadorned instruction for an assignment. But it's possible that the teacher or students will be expecting and wanting to play the game despite the shortened period and are willing to go as far as time allows. By all means, change gears and give them the game. Students are still children and children love to play. Don't we all love to play?

Here's some hard-learned advice about the games: set rules so that the most competitive members don't run away with the game. For example, require everyone to respond at some point, and allow teamwork. Keep it fast-paced and competitive. Offer bonus questions that anyone can answer. (For example, "Who has their library card or card number with them today?" or "Who attended the last track or swim meet?") With these questions, you are also reinforcing the good behaviors in a less didactic way. Most important, use games that today's students find enjoyable. Find out what television shows or video games interest them, and create a competition that has elements of the show or game. It certainly doesn't have to copy the original idea exactly, but using the concept that they enjoy and are familiar with always gains students' attention.

For example, the movie *Napoleon Dynamite* is one that many teens have seen over and over; we hear lines from it repeated in the halls and costumes from the film are designed for Halloween and dances. The movie itself even includes a competition—a student council election that has two very different candidates: one being the pretty and popular blonde cheerleader, and the other being the new kid at school who is a poor male student with only one friend. Create library instruction around the movie's election (see Chapter 8). Form teams of supporters for the candidates. Develop challenges or questions based on the class's real information need or assignment, and the team with the most points or votes at the end of the library instruction wins the election. Students, by their own involvement in the library game, will love the opportunity to change the ending of the movie that they know and love. You can even hang "Vote for Pedro" and "Vote for Summer" posters in your library to add to the theme. It takes a little effort to make the posters and create the game, but you'll be sure to have a huge payoff in student participation and learning.

We Don't Get Many Chances, So We Have to Get It Right the First Time

Teachers are miserly with their class time—with good reason. The precious time allotted for our information literacy instruction needs to fit into the time that is gifted to us. Even if we had more time, we might not be able to fit it into the library schedule.

We need to use our time wisely and prioritize what is most important in our library program because our library media center is everyone's resource; it's not just intended for teaching formal library instruction. If you have space for simultaneous activities to occur in your library, you're very lucky. Otherwise you'll need to survey faculty and staff, have a discussion with administration for support, and do some serious thinking and decision making about what you're able to do best with the tools you have.

The decisions you make are affected by your collaborative partnerships with teachers; teachers should be involved in the library's planning because you will often be team teaching, planning instruction for assignments or research, providing space for projects to be created, and so forth. Ask teachers the important questions that determine what's working and what's not: are you able to conduct a full information literacy lesson during a single class period, or do you need to ask the teacher for more time? Can you justify the amount of time? Can you eliminate or cut some information from topics that the teacher is already covering in class, such as bibliographies and citation or plagiarism and copyright? By planning together, you can decide who will cover which skills and the best method and timing for the instruction.

Can you redesign your space so that instruction and drop-in visits can occur simultaneously? Can you avoid scheduling your time and library space during lunches so that students are free to come in for help or resources? Are your library's hours appropriate, or do you need to lengthen the time the library is open so that patron needs are met? Can you have additional staff or money for the extra hours? Or is it a matter of making your library more teen-friendly and welcoming. Can students listen to music with headphones after school, instant message (IM) their friends during free time, peruse the latest graphic and contemporary novels, or just relax until their next class?

Finally, students judge the library, library staff, and the library's resources at first sight and experience. So much depends on the first impression, and it takes a lot of time to change those poor first impressions. Students are willing and eager to spend time and thought on that which is appealing to them. So let's give it to them. Let them see, feel, and hear what is currently important in their world. To reiterate what I stated earlier, ask the students what they want and what interests them.

Students Need to Evolve Past Information Hunting and Gathering

Students can locate facts about presidents, rodents, chemistry moles, and authors without using more than five brain cells at a time. They've been doing more or less the same thing since second grade. We need to stimulate them into wondering, imagining, designing, defining the how and why of situations so that they develop critical thinking skills to become adept evaluators and analyzers of information. All current educational philosophies emphasize the importance of critical thinking and cognitive learning in developing minds. Students must be both taught and motivated to interact closely with academic puzzles, questions, information, and situations.

No longer should the classroom be a place where knowledge is simply dispensed by an educator. It should be a space where students challenge, test, and determine how to best relate to academic and real-world issues. Today's students, with their structured daily lives, have fewer opportunities for daydreaming and independent decision making that helps them to develop these abilities on their own. It's important that we give them opportunities to make new connections to information and discover ways of approaching situations. Both good and bad habits arise out of need and interest. Provide situations where they can practice applying similar information and knowledge to new situations and guide their minds into good critical-thinking skills.

For instance, we know students can figure out ways to bend the rules without much effort. Let's tap into their natural ability for being resourceful and let them demonstrate those talents in our library. If you haven't been able to collaborate with a certain teacher to create inquiry-based assignments, ask that teacher if you can tweak the assignment (at least for the sake of the library instruction) so that students are asked "why" and "how" instead of "what." Because of time restraints, it's unlikely you'll have time to explore more than a single issue, but you may accomplish two things with this single effort: the students gain the benefit from inquiry-based learning, and the teacher may rethink his assignment when he sees the students' involvement and perhaps come to you for collaboration for the next assignment. It's those small steps that lead to big successes.

Imagine a freshman class coming to the library to search for information for a First Amendment poster assignment. Instead of looking for only the historical facts, legislative wordings, and a few challenges to the amendment, ask students to explain how the First Amendment relates to them as teens and students of your school. You'll probably get some blank stares, and you'll need to prompt them with specific ideas. Ask if anyone is aware of the upcoming trip or event sponsored by your community service club to protest some human rights violations. Some hands may go up. Then ask them how that might relate to the First Amendment. Then move on to the school newspaper and the right to speak about controversial issues. Finally, students should begin offering issues and some complex ideas about related First Amendment concerns such as Internet filtering and the U.S. PATRIOT Act. If not, continue to prompt them until you see them making connections.

Here's another positive outcome of well-planned assignments that include critical thinking: the possibility of plagiarism is greatly lessened when assignments are based on how students interpret and use information. The topic of plagiarism and cheating leads us into the seventh reason library instruction needs to be fun.

They Will Be Taking Care of Us in Our Old Age

We want the leaders and voters of tomorrow to be able to make good decisions that are based on integrity, knowledge, and wisdom. The mention of plagiarism turns every student's head when you suggest that you're going to teach them how to avoid it. By revealing your assumption (true or not) that students plagiarize unintentionally because they don't know how to avoid it allows them to drop their defenses and hear what you have to say. Ethics always have more value than the obvious, and perhaps your students will applaud copyright laws when they understand that our museums, libraries, and bookstores depend on them. Finally, those students who hope to become authors, artists, or other creative types will appreciate that they will be able to earn a living because of copyright laws and those who abide by them.

REFERENCES

Eisenberg, Mike. (2001–2005). *A Big6 Skills Overview* [Online]. Retrieved October 20, 2004, from the Big6 Associates Web site: http://www.big6.com/showcategory.php?cid=6

McKenzie, Jamie. (2004). *The research cycle* [online]. Retrieved October 10, 2004, from http://questioning.org/Q6/research.html

Tell, Carol. (December 1999/January 2000). Generation what? Connecting with today's youth. *Educational Leadership, 57*, p. 4.

Chapter 3

Finding and Using Pop Culture in Our Library Instruction

It's not easy keeping up with trends and fads, but it's homework we must pursue as educators. If our interests don't naturally include popular television, music, and celebrity news, we must discipline ourselves to read, watch, and observe what's new in those areas that interest our students. The effort doesn't have to be exclusive of your normal routine; for example, instead of reading the *New Yorker* while waiting for a dentist appointment, choose *People* or *Seventeen*. Pick up information by eating lunch with young teachers and staff who are tuned in to the latest fads; the stories they tell about students are full of details about teens' interests. Watch *Entertainment Tonight* and read movie and television guides and listings. For the most reliable information about teen interests, talk to teens and listen to them talking to each other on the bus, at the mall, and in your library. Observing and interacting with teens is the most direct way to stay informed and aware of what they enjoy and pursue for entertainment, and it gives you insight into how they prefer to communicate with adults and each other. Students have a lot of stress in their lives, but despite the rapid pace and pressures that they face, they are for the most part idealistic, hardworking, caring, and hopeful about their future. Would any of us trade a minute of a day with them? Probably not, and we certainly can benefit from the energy they bring to our library and our professional life.

How can we keep them curious and engaged while learning with the inclusion of games or pop culture? You might be worried that the additional distraction of the game will detract from what you are teaching. Don't worry a bit. As masters of multitasking, students will naturally be able to handle the additional elements of the interaction and will more likely absorb what they are learning through the game than they will if you just lecture and tell them what they need to know about information. The Kaiser Family Foundation Study, *Generation M: Media in the Lives of 8–18 Year-Olds* (Roberts, Foehr, & Rideout, 2005) describes how our youth spend substantial amounts of time with media, that most kids often use two or more media simultaneously, and that it appears they engage in media multitasking during at least a quarter of their media exposure time. In addition, Roberts and colleagues state, "Anything that takes up that much space in their lives certainly deserves our full attention" (p. 60).

How can we disagree with this research and statement? We see students doing it all at the same time; they are attached to their iPods and cell phones while talking to friends in the halls of our school or working on computers. Why fight it when it's so natural for them?

Mainstream fads and interests that students easily recognize are suggested as themes. Avoid the fads that only a small portion of students at your school find interesting; it's important to have some excitement and buy-in from all students during library instruction, or you might as well go back to scavenger hunts and practice drills for searching your catalog. Take popular culture beyond library instruction and incorporate it into your entire library program by sponsoring events and contests, displaying contemporary posters and news, and providing a teen-friendly atmosphere both physically and in the climate of your library (see Chapter 4). Don't allow a single student to walk away feeling as though the library or library staff is unapproachable.

So what forms of popular culture influence our students, and what are the things we can incorporate into our library instruction? How can we keep up with the fickle and constantly changing pop culture? Take a look at the following ideas. Build on what is offered here or in Chapter 8, or use the ideas to spark your own creativity.

INCORPORATING POP CULTURE INTO YOUR PROGRAM

Reality TV
Movies
Music
Sports
Games
Books and literature
Popular teen hangouts

Reality TV

No matter how you were introduced to reality TV, chances are that you are hooked on at least a show or two. Today, it seems that more shows are reality shows than not (not that reality has anything to do with it). Just this past weekend while watching a cable channel, there was a sixty-second reality commercial with three people rushing around a department store to locate a list of a sponsor's brand-name items. They cut back to the commercial between show breaks. Pretty innovative way to market consumer goods—it grabs the viewer's attention, and natural curiosity motivates them to stay tuned to see if they complete their task.

Although most reality TV consists of a competition of some sort, not all are appropriate for the high school classroom. For example, the dating shows put too much emphasis on relationships and physical appearance and might cause embarrassment, insecurity, or inappropriate responses from students. But with some amount of creativity and tweaking, most reality TV adapts to a game of library instruction, and those with challenges or competitions among players work especially well (see Chapter 8 for specific presentations and adaptations). Because *Survivor* and *The Amazing Race* include challenges that test participants' knowledge, effort, tenacity, and skills, they adapt easily to information literacy instruction. Break up your class into teams or "tribes" and challenge them to be the highest-scoring team that wins the big prize at the end of the game. Build your instruction into the presentation and create and add challenges whenever it seems appropriate to reinforce an idea or strategy. Use the class assignment for topics to search, and have students demonstrate the various methods of finding useful and credible information.

A simple and fun way to surprise students and make them wonder what you're up to is to post images of Ian or Jenna of *Survivor* fame, Donald Trump and one of his new apprentices, or a team from *The Amazing Race* on shelving, walls, or doors around the library. If nothing else, students ask questions about why those images are in the library, conversations about what they enjoy on television enlightens you, and you'll undoubtedly be given suggestions for other images or themes.

Movies

Movie characters and themes are easy to integrate into library instruction, and movies like those from the Harry Potter or Lord of the Rings series work great because the quests pursued in the movies, the books on which they are based, and your own library instruction provide many opportunities for making correct choices that lead to gaining knowledge. You can break up the class into groups that represent the elves, dwarfs, and hobbits for the Lord of the Rings, or into the Slytherin, Griffndor, or Hufflepuff houses for Harry Potter. The aim is for students to collect points by correctly answering or completing questions and challenges along the way to become the winners of the game. Give prizes to everyone—larger ones to the winners and small tokens to everyone else. Challenges don't need to stay in theme of the movie; we must not lose sight of the fact that information literacy and research skills are the main objective. If appropriate, however, some challenges could involve locating a book written by Tolkien, finding out how many volumes of Harry Potter the library owns, and explaining how to reserve a copy. Keep students motivated by engaging both their minds and bodies—require a representative from each group to pull a specific book from the shelf and show it to you; this reinforces successful catalog searching, use of the Dewey decimal system, and navigation of your library. One word of warning: many teens who have seen the movies will not have read the books, so stay true to the movie (unless you've based your theme on the book) in building challenges and quests. But what a great opportunity to spark the interest of students in reading the books and discovering the differences between them and the movies.

Music

No matter what year it is, music remains one of the most age-specific media that exists. Is there anyone who can't recall exactly where they were and what they were doing by hearing a few bars of a song from their high school days? Even though other generations know and like music from the past, the music of the day is what defines the youth culture. Not all teens like all the music of the day, but you can bet that they recognize most and know who the artist is. Of course, there are limitations to the music we can have blaring down the school hallways, but why not lure students into the library by playing some of their favorite music between bells? As long as the lyrics are appropriate for public consumption, it's just another hook to bring them in and make them feel comfortable. Most students listen to music at home while doing homework, reading, playing video games, and communicating with friends; having background music or noise don't seem to affect their performance. Headphones are a must when students get down to work, however; individual rights end where someone else's rights begin. If an assignment allows for a music theme, teach Boolean logic by searching for lyrics (but you might not want to call it "Boolean"). Have students locate information about their favorite band as long as they use truncation punctuation, search the name as a phrase, and use a newspaper database. In addition, music provides an opportunity to discuss copyright issues. Ask the class how copyright laws affect a musician's ability to earn a living and what might happen to the wide variety of musical choices if musicians were forced to work at other jobs instead of spending their time and energy to make music. Reinforce the idea that we want to reward talented people so that we reap the benefits of their creativity and talent.

Sports

Sports are a natural fit as a theme, and whether your school is crazy over football, soccer, or field hockey, it is certain to bring out the competitive spirit. The stereotypical athlete who may not be interested in academics may be encouraged to go beyond what's expected to demonstrate her ability to win in an athletically themed game. If the class assignment involves world history or a related topic and the project is fairly open-ended, you can demonstrate search strategies and base challenges on locating sports information about the first Olympics or the hostage situation at the 1972 Olympics in Munich. If you use a topic such as dodgeball that is a sport, a game, and a movie, you'll be sure to have everyone tuned in. Form dodgeball teams and have points awarded as hits, dodges, or any other terms that fit the theme. Boolean strategies aren't nearly as scary when students use topics that interest them or are interesting in a surprising way.

Games

Games such as Uh-Gi-Oh! , Dungeons and Dragons, or Magic really grab the boys' attention. Although older boys were the original collectors and players, it seems that younger boys (middle school and younger) are now getting involved. It's a good idea to talk to a few boys at your school and ask if they'd be interested in the topic or if they have other ideas—the last thing you want to do is to insult them by using what they perceive as a babyish theme. Both girls and boys might be interested in the beanbag tossing game of Corn Hole (it may just be a Midwestern phenomena, but it sure is popular). Remember that it doesn't really matter what the theme of the game is—it can be adapted if you set up the presentation to reflect the theme. Name the groups with some related name, use the lingo associated, and fit in what you need them to learn as always. You don't have to (and usually won't want to) create strategies using the game theme. All students aren't in the same place developmentally, and although many may be able to use their critical-thinking skills to adapt the "pop culture" themes and strategies to their assigned research, some have a more difficult time making the connection. Although the hook of pop culture is intended to grab their attention and to teach strategies that they can remember, students need to find the information related to their assignment and will be happy to get authentic search strategies from you concerning the topics at hand.

Books and Literature

Books and literature are probably the easiest to adapt and fit into library instruction, and you can stay "in theme" for your entire instruction. For example, if a class is coming to the library to research characters, themes, symbolism, and settings of *Lord of the Flies*, you can use the topic to demonstrate search strategies and create challenges that allow them to search for exactly what they need for their assignment. Perhaps you can get them to think critically and creatively beyond what they think they need as well. Depending on the level of your students, you can challenge them to locate the symbolism associated with Piggy's glasses or what the Beast represents in the book. Any title chosen for high school analysis and study provides plenty of opportunity for fast-paced and interesting information literacy instruction.

Popular Teen Hangouts

Malls and shopping centers, arcades, amusement parks, or many other places that amuse teens make wonderful themes for instruction. Whether the winner(s) walk away with a prize at the end of the game from earning the most arcade tickets, the shoppers leave with prizes from the most mall certificates earned, or amusement park patrons vie for a free front-of-the-line pass for their favorite ride, everyone has a good time trying to win. And you know that what they are really winning is knowledge and skills.

Finally, use the teens in your life as your personal focus groups. Ask your students, children, grandchildren, or neighbors about movies, music, books, and fashion that interest them. Going directly to those who are creating the current popular culture should provide you with the most credible information that you can use in your libraries.

REFERENCE

Roberts, Donald F., Foehr, Ulla G., & Rideout, Victoria. *Generation M: Media in the Lives of 8–18 Year-Olds*. A Kaiser Family Foundation Study [online]. Retrieved May 7, 2005, from http://www.kff.org/entmedia/entmedia030905pkg.cfm

Chapter 4

Putting the Cool into Your Library to Inspire This Generation

As stated in Chapter 3, students judge the library, library staff, and the library's resources at first sight and by their past experiences. So much depends on the first impression because it takes a lot more time to change those impressions.

WHAT WORKS AND WHAT THEY WANT

If your library is open for a time before and after school, you can easily find out what happens in the library when students come in on their own without a class. Become a voyeur (you can always argue that information seeking is part of your job). Watch what they are doing on the computers and see if they are blogging, e-mailing, IMing, shopping, reading, or locating information about entertainment or current news. It's especially helpful to know if they are doing homework, working on a project, searching the library catalog, using subscription databases, and so forth. If something looks interesting, stop and ask about it. Even if you know the answer, go for the dialogue to discover more. Consider asking these types of questions: Are you finding what you need? Which IM service do you use? I thought we had an IM blocking filter—do you IM here all the time? What Blog is that? Did you know that we have a book Blog for our library? Do you use our school's e-mail or a different e-mail service with your friends? Do you ever e-mail your teachers? What do you think about our computers? Are they fast enough? What about our Web site—is it easy to navigate?

Try your hardest to talk to students using your curiosity approach and not your adult person-in-charge personality. You'll usually find students to be very honest and truthful and to enjoy the interaction. Try not to interrupt someone with the panicky "got to get this done" look, however, and try not to wear the person out with too many questions.

19

Respond to the feedback by creating new services, passing ideas on to administration and the technology department, and telling students that the changes are a result of their feedback. The ideas from your interaction with students will also help you plan your budget for the following year. Do you need more or fewer databases, promotional materials, or special interest contests, for example?

Even though most school librarians are solo with maybe a library assistant or clerk to help out, it's most important to get and stay involved with professional organizations. If your school doesn't offer professional days for workshops, meetings, or conferences during the school day, you can still find some after-school meetings and workshops to keep your knowledge up-to-date. Many libraries belong to regional library consortiums that provide resource sharing, networking, technology consultation, and professional development opportunities. Despite many legitimate reasons why you don't have time or money to spend on meetings and outside activities, you will find that what you bring back from meetings, workshops, and conferences is far too valuable to miss. It is worthwhile to convince your administration of this by demonstrating to the faculty what you have learned at your school's in-services or by offering faculty and staff professional development workshops throughout the school year or summer.

ATMOSPHERE

Talking Is Required in the Library

When I first arrived at St. Ursula Academy eight years ago, I placed a sign in the library that set the tone for change. I wanted the library to become a place where ideas were exchanged and challenged, where information was sought not only from traditional sources but also from each other, and where students wanted to hang out. The big sign "Talking Is Required in the Library" was the first signage I added, and it hung near the door. I didn't really expect much attention from it, but students did notice and pointed it out to friends and classmates. Being new, I was frequently tested and students often pointed to the sign (my own words) as an excuse to discuss plans for Friday night and news about their friends. I always replied, in a friendly way, that group work for assignments and talking about books and readings, and school-related things was what the sign implied. I reminded them that the freedom to talk and discuss ends where someone else's right to study and learn in an appropriate setting begins. I'd end the session with something light like, "So where are you going on Friday night?" or "Have fun but be safe." Students were willing to live with that explanation. They seemed to appreciate that the atmosphere was somehow different in their library now, and I wanted them to realize that I wasn't just a light fixture or piece of furniture without ears and a brain. I listened to what they were saying. Discussion hasn't stopped yet with regard to the sign or their plans for Friday nights.

FACILITIES

Many school libraries are small, perhaps two classrooms combined for the library, and it's likely that you don't have room for comfy couches and reading corners. But just placing a rocking chair near the newspapers and print magazines and some beanbag chairs that students can move around the library is an appreciated effort to create atmosphere and invite patrons to sit, relax, and read a little. Don't discourage students from sitting on the floor and sprawling. It should be the activity that determines whether they are asked to change their position or behavior—if they are earnestly involved in reading, studying, homework, or writing, let them hang from the ceiling. But if they are talking loudly about their new shoes and playing solitaire on the computer, it's fair to ask them to take their socializing out in the hall or to be quieter. Then make a mental note about the type of shoes that they all think are cool to use as a search example during instruction.

School-related work should take priority before school, during lunches, and after school so that students who earnestly need to use a computer are able to work. However, discouraging those students who want to e-mail friends, shop, check out the weather and travel news, and catch up on celebrity gossip will make teens reluctant to think of the library as anything but an academic place. Provide headphones so that they can listen to music and let them feel comfortable.

Open your blinds to let natural light in, hang international flags and bright posters that you change periodically, and add color in any way you can. Attempts to make your space inviting to teens will pay off. It's hard to provide appealing library services to teens if they aren't there to receive them.

Figure 4.1. Students appreciate all efforts to create a comfortable and inviting facility.

SERVICES

If your library facility is small, be resolved to have a large, robust library program to make up for it. If you can't rely on the physical appearance of your library to prove its worth to students, parents, and administration, then create a bustling atmosphere with so much activity and interaction that no one notices the ugly carpet, dreary walls, or close quarters.

How many times have students (or even teachers) asked about a book or piece of information and started by stating, "You won't have it here," or "I know our library is too small." Don't those phrases send shivers up your spine? Take the vow to never allow your patrons to leave the library without the information they need or a promise to find it or find out how to make it available to them.

This type of situation offers a perfect time to describe how technology has changed what a library is and how it operates. Our library's walls are only an illusion with today's technology and library networks and consortiums. Tell every class that comes to your library for instruction and every student who asks for information that your ability to locate information is boundless and that you can help her find what she needs directly or through other libraries, librarians, or information sources. Always, always, always emphasize that librarians, aka library gods or goddesses, are the most important library tools. Remind them that despite having gone to library school and working in a library that we, too, can become disoriented and in need of direction whenever we enter a library for the first time. Compare trying to use a new library like getting lost when you're driving—you don't allow not knowing which way to turn stop you from finding out where to go. You stop and ask for directions. It saves time and trouble overall. Using a librarian is like asking for driving directions—it's the librarian's environment, and she or he is best able to direct you to what you need.

Our students are lucky that they live in this information- and technology-rich age. Use their desire for instant gratification and quick results to demonstrate how they have advantages in locating information today. Remind them that when you went to high school, there was no Internet, e-mail, or, in some cases, even copiers. Describe the long physical process of using print materials and indexes instead of full-text databases. You'll see and feel them sympathizing with the old and rigorous method of finding information that you remember. Discuss how fast and simple accessing information is today because computers and the Internet can provide us with an article days before the same article in the print magazine arrives in our mailbox. Emphasize that the delivery method is the only difference in the two formats and how wonderful it is that we can have a perfectly clean, non-dog-eared or food-stained copy for ourselves. This is a good thing for teachers to hear over and over. (How many teachers in your school still require students to cut out newspaper and magazine articles no matter how much you've tried to convince them that the electronic version isn't a "copy" but the original article with a different delivery method?) Purposely show envy over the ease at which they search, locate, and gather information compared with how it was done in the past. However, do point out that all this access to information isn't easy at all if they don't understand how information is created, they don't have useful research skills, the network is down, their computer is broken, or their little brother or sister is hogging the computer.

COLLECTION

Typically, school libraries use every inch of their facility to provide what students need and want. Be certain to include an up-to-date fiction collection that is largely what students have requested or what has been reviewed to be what teens are devouring. Use a suggestion box for those shy students or ask them when they are checking out a book what other books they'd like. In addition to a collection that supports your curriculum, try to offer your students audio books, graphic novels, gay teen and social issues literature, 'zines and ezines, primary resources such as autobiographies, memoirs, and diaries, and all the award-winning and worthy fiction and nonfiction that you can find and afford. When teachers or students mention a title they'd like, buy it immediately. It's likely that you don't have a huge budget and that it has been shriveling in the past years, but always budget enough money to cover personal and immediate need requests. Quick responses to requests are always appreciated by students, teachers, and staff. You'll be surprised how quickly they begin to depend on you for resources.

Graphic novels are currently the hottest books on our shelves, and just when you think you have the latest, one of the ganga or manga fans will ask why the library doesn't have the newest release of a series. It's a constant struggle to provide what students want with the money we have for all the library's programming and services, but we need to continue trying.

To house a very current collection in limited space, you also need to weed constantly. Get rid of fiction that has lost its appeal over the years, whether its award-winning or not, and always replace or permanently remove yellowing and ugly books.

LIBRARY INSTRUCTION

It's good policy to acknowledge student's comfort and skills with technology tools. Ask them for suggestions about how to make searching more efficient, and pass those tips on to others through your instruction. Don't dismiss students' suggestions even if they are unsophisticated or even incorrect. Build on what they offer and use it to move to a more clearly defined strategy or example. With an American history class, you might ask how to locate information about the Trail of Tears. Students will first look at you like you're crazy, and reply, "type 'Trail of Tears'." You might reply that that's a good place to start, but what are you trying to tell the computer? Do you want trail of tears as a phrase with the three words together exactly as they are typed, or do you want the word "trail" anywhere in the record and the word "tears" anywhere in the record as long as both terms are there? And what different results might you get from either strategy? What about the "of" in the search? Inform the students about how those prepositions and articles can confuse a search engine and result in strange hits. Give them an example of how the word "trail" may result in information about hiking trails in the Rocky Mountains or how "tears" could point to information about tear ducts, sad movies or books, or the verb that means shredding or ripping. You will begin to see two types of reactions:

1. a more attentive posture—that their brains are starting to engage or

2. an eyes-glazed-over and annoyed posture—that they don't want to be bothered with worrying about how the computer reacts to their strategy because they know they get some results from typing it in either way.

It's time to move on and describe the same strategies with a topic of more interest to them. Take the name "Britney Spears" and ask students to think about how the computer views the words. If you type in the first and last name as a phrase, you should retrieve information or results about that specific person or persons with the same name. But if you type in "Britney" as a term and "Spears" as a second term connected with an "and," you might retrieve information about Britney Jones, Smith, and so on who grows or cooks asparagus spears.

Give them a chance to try it out. They will undoubtedly say that they got results about the real Britney Spears at the top of their results list. Concur, but ask them to go further down the list until they get to stranger things that aren't at all related. They'll agree that this happens but that they won't usually look further when they find what they need on the first page of results. Reply that this is because you know who Britney is and can recognize that the information is definitely about her. But if you were searching for someone or something that you don't know anything about, how will you know for sure if that is the information you need? If time permits, take the lesson another step and ask them to search only for an image of Britney Spears. You not only reinforce the search strategy, but you will be informing about the image option with most databases or search engines. They are also learning while entertaining themselves with something that interests them. Depending on your audience, use pop or country music, sport, or entertainment celebrities to achieve the same results.

Now you have their attention and have convinced them that things are a bit trickier than they first thought. You can get back to the Trail of Tears topic. Depending on time and the reaction from your students, you could also bring up the topic of synonyms or related terms for searching may help them locate information that they need. At some point, be sure to remind them that learning this will save them tons of time that they can use to chat and talk to their friends (just not during class time). Confirm at this point that your intention is not to make them master researchers but to find the information they need for their assignment so that they can move on with their lives more quickly.

The popular culture names and themes that you work into lessons keeps students engaged. If you use Abraham Lincoln instead of Britney Spears in the former task, it's likely that several students will tune out before you complete the lesson. Students respond to the instructional style that makes learning enjoyable, and they will prove that to you when you observe them demonstrating skillful searching of your electronic catalog and online proprietary databases, choosing high-quality information for assignments and coming back to visit from college telling you that their college instructors and librarians are impressed with what they know about research and information.

For an added twist, use the same pop culture themes and terms just discussed, but flip the strategy and challenge students to perform searches that will be certain *not* to locate good and useful information. Students will need to understand and have the same knowledge, but they will stretch their minds in the exercise to achieve opposite results. Allow students to demonstrate and show others how not to do it.

LIFELONG LEARNERS

For us to create lifelong learners, it's necessary to create both information-literate users and literature lovers. Define the term "literature" loosely as both fiction and nonfiction, not restricted to the classics, award winners, or best-sellers, and consider how it takes to read any type of material to continue learning and growing.

For classes that integrate books into their curriculum and after you've discussed the details of your plan with the teacher, allow the class to sit back and relax with book talks. For example, use book talks with students as part of their formal library instruction. You can sneak in information about publishing, copyright, and plagiarism in an informal atmosphere along with the book talks. When they arrive in the library, have a selection of books surrounding you from which they can choose before they leave or tell them that you can help them find similar books. Depending on the teacher's wishes, choose fiction, nonfiction, biography, and autobiography. It's best to use titles that are contemporary with attractive covers to pull them in. Let them settle around you as you begin to describe and read from a few of the books. Prepare a collection of books with bookmarked passages that will peak their curiosity or an especially dramatic part that encourages them to read the whole book.

Although you may be tempted to spend the entire time reading to your students, be sure to save enough time for them to select their book and to help those who have a harder time choosing. Most of the books from which you read will disappear immediately, so it is advisable that you have many more books selected and prepared for the next class. Also, encourage students to tell about books that they've read and loved and would recommend to their peers for the assignment. Allow students to exchange ideas, titles, and authors. If recommended titles aren't in your library collection, you can promise to order those books or help locate them through the public library's catalog or on Amazon. No high school student is too old or sophisticated for book talks. They love the down time, and you'll find that your students are more attentive and quiet than you've thought possible.

Look for ways at your school and in your library to promote reading for pleasure. Sponsor a quarterly book talk session or use National Library Week to offer a "books and bagels" session that combines book talks and food. Figure out when it works best at your school. Perhaps before school, during lunches, or after school are the only opportunities for students to have free time, but teens appreciate the effort—and the free food—anytime. If your library sponsors a book club for students, that's perfect, but if someone else moderates the book club, offer to sponsor it by paying for food and refreshments. Perhaps the cash from library fines can fund the sponsorship. Ask for recognition on club signs or T-shirts.

SPECIAL ACTIVITIES

Although Teen Read Week, Right to Read Week, National Library Week, and National Poetry Month are perfect times to present new programs, any time is the right time for you to lure students into your library. Following are programs that have worked and are useful starting point for even more creative programming.

Spontaneous Bursts of Reading (SBOR)

Schedule ten minutes (or as much time as your school will spare) for required reading sessions that occur at random intervals, daily, all week long. Warn teachers before that week and make the necessary materials available to them. Use the PA system to announce the SBOR. Classes should stop immediately for the reading. Teachers or an assigned student reads to the class from a book for the allotted time. If your city has an "On the Same Page" reading program, use it and borrow enough copies for every classroom (check copyright laws before copying chapters).

Library and Lunch Chats

Invite students to bring their brown-bag lunches (provide cookies or candy as dessert) to the library once a month to enjoy a discussion about a preset topic of interest. Choose a current news topic, a sports figure, a book author, a celebrity, hot fashions or trends, or anything that interests your students. It's a great opportunity to connect their popular culture to the library and to interact in an informal way with your students. You'll find many returning time after time for the social time.

Library Tea

Spread the tablecloths and bring out the teapots and china (or ask everyone to bring their favorite mug or cup). This setting is a lure to pull teachers and students into the library for an unusual (and somewhat fancier) event. You can offer book talks or you can display new materials. Have plenty of handouts or freebies to give to participants. Refreshments help create the atmosphere for friendly bonding. If a formal setting isn't your style, have a "Picnic in the Stacks" instead.

Book Match Contest

Students match teachers to their favorite book. Send a multiple-choice quiz to homerooms for students to complete. Students exchange and correct the quizzes, and those with the highest scores are the winners. Homeroom teachers sign the winners' quizzes and students bring them to the library to receive their prizes.

Become Your Favorite Book Character for a Day

All students and teachers love dress-down days. To make it more fun and appropriate for National Library Week, have participants dress as a book character. It's likely that you'll see Harry Potter, geishas, Macbeth, and Alice in Wonderland walking your halls. Photograph the individuals holding the book that involves the character they are portraying and display them with a summary of the book. The recognition might give positive feedback to some students who don't normally receive attention.

Parents' Night in the Library

Involve parents in your events. Create a program called "How to Become a Savvy Library User in 90 Minutes" for an evening session and invite parents to spend some "non-parenting" time in their children's library and school. Parents love to know what resources are available for their children and getting a leg up on using technology and information resources themselves. Focus the evening on locating information that should be of interest to them—search for travel, parenting, and health information from the same resources that their children use for school assignments. Don't assume that they are information-literate themselves; provide information about publishing, Web versus proprietary or scholarly information, or any tips that will aid them in locating worthwhile information. In addition to providing a pleasant program for parents, you'll create a relationship with some important stakeholders in your community who may become more supportive of the library and its needs.

Faculty and Staff Book Club

Create an adult book club for socializing and discussing books. Survey your faculty and staff to determine when and where to meet and how often. Some public libraries provide book discussion kits that include multiple copies of a title and discussion topics and questions. Ask members to provide suggestions for books. You can ask an English teacher to moderate the discussion. Provide refreshments or organize a potluck to emphasis the relaxed, social atmosphere.

Book Making Workshop

Allow students to make their own book out of handmade paper or wrapping paper so they can give them as gifts or use for as their own journal or scrapbook. It sounds complicated, but many books are very simple projects with inexpensive materials. It's not difficult to locate an artsy or crafty person at school or in your community to present the session; most people love to share a hobby or interest. Ask your art teacher to present or suggest someone else, and make certain that you are there to welcome students after school for a couple of hours of creative fun.

'Zine- or Ezine-Making Workshop

'Zines are publications (often self-published) on any topic under the sun. They can be a few pages handwritten and stapled together or a hundred pages published in color by a printing service. Blogs or ezines are the electronic version of the 'zine. Students love to voice their opinions by either creating or reading 'zines. It seems as though they usually appeal to those students who like edgier things with a political or literary side. Most schools already have literary magazines that are a good example of a 'zine, and students can use their personal interests and creative sides to make their own. Check out the title *From A to Zine: Building a Winning Zine Collection in Your Library* by Julie Bartel (2004). The book not only describes how to build a 'zine collection (with Salt Lake City's collection and experiences as an example) but how to provide programs with them.

Create a Bookmark Contest

This contest promotes your school library. Have students submit their original and creative entries to you and form a small committee to judge them. Suggest a theme and scan and use the winning bookmark(s) to distribute in the library, at an open house, and at parent events. Working with an art teacher to promote the contest ensures many good entries.

Used Book Sale

Donated books or discards that don't fit your needs are often difficult to dispose of. Instead of tossing your books out or giving them away, sell them to students, teachers, and parents. Invite students, teachers and staff to clean off their bookshelves and to donate to the library's used book sale. Recruit parent or student volunteers to organize, publicize, and run the sale. Reward your donors and volunteers with recognition or with free used books. Don't charge much for the used books, or you'll be dragging them back into the library. Instead of labeling books, organize them into dime and quarter tables and provide bags for a price that they can fill up with as many books as possible. Use the cash that you reap for your library instruction prizes.

Quote of the Day

Read a daily quote during announcements that focuses on books, libraries, or education as a part of morning announcements during National Library Week. Award prizes to the first person to respond via e-mail with a correct source (it doesn't have to be the identical source that you used). Offer categories for both the faculty and staff members. Look for quotes using a simple strategy either from a search engine or from your databases—you want students to be rewarded for participating.

Reel Librarians

Offer movies that feature librarians cast in major roles and popcorn after school during National Library Week. *Party Girl* and *The Gun in Betty Lou's Handbag* are fun movies with contemporary themes (make certain of the rating before you announce them). There are many Web sites with lists of movies with librarians as characters.

Movies with Librarians Quiz

Test your students and staff's knowledge about the roles of librarians in movies. As with the quote contest, the first person to respond via e-mail with the correct source is the winner.

Coffee House

Coffee isn't required, but poetry or literature is. Have students bring their original works or allow them to read their favorite poet's or friend's piece. Serve refreshments and create a coffee house atmosphere with background music and candles. Perhaps you can get your principal to agree to have a dress-down day for participants who come dressed in coffee house–style garb.

Poetry Slam

Students love writing and performing poetry, and the slam takes the coffee house event one step further. The dramatic presentation of the poetry is as (or more) important as the content in a slam. The performer and the audience play an equally important role in the event. Pick a panel of judges randomly from the audience, and the audience reacts strongly to the judges' scores. Performances are normally original works, but you can adapt the slam for many categories. It's important that participants understand that slams are in no way a serious literary competition, and the best poetry doesn't always win. Usually it's the crowd-pleasing presentation or theme that runs away with the prizes. Slams are being recognized as an option to involve teens with literature. Take a look at ALA's slam rules at http://www.ala.org/ala/yalsa/teenreading/trw/trw2003/wayscelebrate.htm or the National Poetry Slam Incorporated rules http://www.poetryslam.com/index.htm.

MAKING THE LIBRARY RELEVANT TO STUDENTS' LIVES

Finally, without the help and cooperation of teachers, our students might not find the time to come to the library no matter how much you offer them and how much they'd like to come. Bus and ride schedules, after-school activities, and work prevent many students from reaping the benefits of what your library can provide.

One of the hardest roles of a school librarian is the collaboration needed to integrate the library program fully into the curriculum. If you've had limited success with approaching individual teachers and campaigning for more involvement with classes, it may be time to approach administration and your curriculum committee (of which you should be a member) with a plan that's dependent on collaboration with teachers. The plan would theoretically ensure that your graduates leave your school information literate and with research and technology skills. Of course, becoming information literate is a lifelong pursuit, especially in our era of quickly changing technologies and media, but to have a level of information literacy that prepares students for college and life beyond our walls is a worthy and doable goal. (See Chapters 5 and 6 for details about getting your school to buy in to your plan.)

REFERENCE

Julie Bartel. (2004). *From A to Zine : Building a Winning Zine Collection in Your Library*. Chicago, IL: American Library Association.

Chapter 5

The Big Buy-in from Administrators and Teachers

It takes several separate steps to create a schoolwide information literacy and research program. To attempt to create new and engaging information literacy instruction and a schoolwide information literacy and research model and to get all administrators, teachers, and students to love your idea and to make it work in a single step is overly ambitious for both you and your school. Break your plan into smaller steps and tackle it one piece at a time (see Chapter 6 for an example of one school's experience). Let the stakeholders adapt to the initial step before moving on to the next. The steps fall in a natural order:

1. Research and understand information literacy and define it for your school.

2. Create a sequence of information literacy and research skills for each grade (we call our sequence and plan a Graded Course of Study).

3. Have your new sequence of skills or Graded Course of Study approved by your school's decision makers.

4. Develop information literacy and research instruction using pop culture based on your Graded Course of Study.

5. Initiate your new instruction and evaluate its success and weaknesses.

6. Continue to improve and adapt your instruction as needed.

7. Create a schoolwide information literacy and research model and plan. This will have to be integrated or at least correlated with the school curriculum and probably should be developed with a faculty curriculum advisory group.

8. Present the plan to administration and the curriculum committee members.

9. Initiate the information literacy and research model in your school.

10. Seek out feedback concerning the model.

11. Improve and adapt the model as needed.

DEFINING INFORMATION LITERACY

You can become immersed in the topic of information literacy in various ways. You can begin at college level with the Association of College and Research Libraries (ACRL; http://acrl.org), a division of the American Library Association (ALA), to understand how higher education defines and takes on the task of information literacy. Because our graduating seniors are their first-year students, there is quite of bit of common interest. Or go straight to the American Association of School Librarian's (AASL) site (http://www. ala.org/ala/aasl/aaslindex.htm) where you'll have a direct track to information literacy for schools. You can also choose to begin with the skills and knowledge your students have when they arrive at your school, examine existing research models, and then find a starting place that will satisfy your school's needs. There is no single correct method of approaching information literacy, and most likely it will involve many methods. Your relationship with information literacy will be a combination of multidirectional interests and approaches that combine what your students know now with what they will need to know to succeed in your high school as well as in college and beyond.

Many organizations and individuals provide philosophies, research models, and advice for the promotion of information literacy. Our education and relationship with information literacy is infinite and dynamic. Take a look at the resources that follow to begin your information literacy quest or for information that will help you enhance it.

Information Literacy Resources

- **The Association of College and Research Libraries (ACRL) Information Literacy Competency Standards for Higher Education:** http://www.ala.org/ala/acrl/acrlstandards/informationliteracycompetency.htm

- **The American Association of School Librarians (AASL) Information Literacy:** http://www.ala.org/aaslTemplate.cfm?Section=aaslinfolit

- **AASL Resource Guides for School Library Media Program Development:** http://www.ala.org/aaslTemplate.cfm?Section=resourceguides&Template=/ContentManagement/ContentDisplay.cfm&ContentID=15288

- **The National Forum on Information Literacy:** http://www.infolit.org/

CREATE A GRADED COURSE OF STUDY

1. Begin researching your state's, district's, or school's literacy standards and research models and compare the information to your school's curriculum and

needs. Compare and contrast them to the ALA's (1998a) *Information Power* or *Information Literacy Standards for Student Learning* (ALA, 1998b).

2. Draw from past bibliographic instruction and the research models that you've used or that you locate in professional literature. Examine similarities and common goals in the information literacy standards and models and align them with your school's goals and standards for specific content areas.

3. Look for information from academic librarians who present and discuss issues concerning their incoming freshmen and the skills and knowledge that they'd like them to possess about libraries, information, and information seeking before they arrive on their doorsteps.

4. Consider copyright and plagiarism issues that involve not only students but all of your school's stakeholders.

5. Finally, develop a specific plan for meeting the objectives and goals that you think are most important for each grade level in your school (see Chapter 6). Consider your school's current classes, proposed classes and changes to classes, teachers, and typical and atypical students.

GRADED COURSE OF STUDY APPROVAL

If you walk into your principal's office and blurt out that you're planning to use the *Survivor* television show to teach library instruction, it's not likely that you'll get much buy-in from administration and ultimately teachers. (In fact, you might be exiled out of your school to a deserted island.) As long as you can demonstrate that standards and curriculum needs are being met, however, it's likely and appropriate that the style will be your own to develop.

Principals don't generally have the interest or time to worry about the details of each lesson plan in schools, so prepare and present only what she or he needs to know. Develop (or redevelop) a Graded Course of Study based on standards and information literacy expectations and present the course of study to the curriculum committee, departments, and administration. It's much later that you will add the popular culture themes to strengthen and add flavor to your instruction.

Approval from your school's administration is a necessary step, and you should proceed no further without the nod. But after creating a well-researched and formulated plan, it will likely be approved by your administration and curriculum group so that you can move on to the implementation stage. That's the most difficult part. There is no promise that you'll have teachers lining up at the library door waiting to collaborate with you or begging you to help their students to become information literate. Your plan is only the beginning in a lengthy process of integrating library instruction into the curriculum.

GRADE LEVELS AND NEEDS

Freshmen are the single most important class to target, and you should spend a lot of time creating programs for them. Not only do they need to become oriented to your library and its rules and achieve the information literacy and research skills levels that are appropriate for their grade level, they must feel comfortable with and learn to depend on what you and your library provide for them. It's necessary for you to win their trust and engage them as quickly as possible. Freshmen enter high school at the eighth-grade knowledge and maturity level but without the security that they achieved as upperclassmen at their previous schools. Even if they don't admit that they are nervous and unsure about new teachers, buildings, peers, and experiences, it is obvious in their posture and in what they do and say (or don't do and don't say). They almost always bring the same habits and learning methods that they used in their former school and keep their fingers crossed that they work in high school. They don't in most cases. High school curriculum that moves rapidly and challenges even the best students quickly demonstrates to freshmen that improved methods of learning and studying are needed. What better timing than in those moments of insecurity when they are beginning a new class or have just been handed a new assignment and are faced with locating information to assimilate into their project? Watch the freshmen enter the library with either cocky attitudes or preset negative expectations and immediately demonstrate what your library and library services offer to begin building a working relationship with each of them. What better way to gain their attention and demonstrate that high school isn't so bad than by making learning fun for them?

DEVELOP INFORMATION LITERACY AND RESEARCH INSTRUCTION

With your Graded Course of Study in one hand, your school's curriculum guide or list of classes (and the respective grade levels) and some pop culture trends and themes in the other, you are ready to begin creating exciting information literacy instruction that your students will love. Adapt the ideas presented in earlier chapters or recreate the instruction in Chapter 8 for each level of students in your school.

It's tempting to be overly ambitious with all the creative ideas you'll have concerning pop culture, but by focusing on creating and implementing the instruction one level or grade at a time, you'll have some experience before moving on to the next level. Adaptations of your initial instruction can easily be used with other levels. You may discover that another level is better suited for that style or game. Don't get so caught up with the game that your instruction and information becomes secondary. Remember that your purpose is to engage the students in the subject rather than just have fun.

It takes consistent reinforcement of information literacy instruction and skills to develop information-literate students. With that in mind, begin with the younger students who will remain in your school for several more years and whom you'll be able to watch develop and grow under your new program. Initiate upper grades instruction after the groundwork is in place with the younger students. Follow these steps to begin your instruction:

1. Create both a visual and an interactive game and presentation for your formal instruction. PowerPoint works well because you can insert audio, animation, challenges or quests, along with the important information points that you are teaching. Make your slides attractive and "in theme." Avoid dense text on a projected presentation or handout because it tends to dull students' senses. Only provide a starting point for your discussion and then allow the energy to direct the instruction and interaction. The best thing that can happen is that there is so

much appropriate participation and so many questions that you need to interject the "one more question/answer rule" or ask the teacher for additional time.

2. Provide handouts of your presentation to the teacher for absent students. Or you can post the PowerPoint presentation to your Web site for student review. Without the discussion and student interaction, much will be missing from the presentation, and it most likely will not be beneficial as a complete tutorial.

3. Create Web-based project and assignment pages that focus students' research on the recommended and most appropriate resources for their topic and assignment in addition to (or instead of) a formal instruction. Add a link to the teacher's assignment page, and students may have everything they need for an assignment. Post those pages on the Web so that students with computers at home have 24/7 access. (Take a look at some examples in Chapter 8 or at http://www.saintursula.org/library/projects/.) You may become very busy with requests from teachers targeted for class instruction as well as those who love the idea of project pages because they allow students to research more independently and successfully. Fear not—once you have a template for the project pages, it is only the research for each topic or assignment that takes time.

4. Go beyond your own school library's resources (catalog, databases, CD-ROMs, Web sites you've located and reviewed, etc.) when preparing instruction or project and assignment pages for older students. Offer links to your public library system, academic library catalogs and resources, and other electronic resources and Web sites that are available to your patrons online. Finally, in addition to the information resources, add links to sites that offer help with citing and bibliographies, and your Internet site evaluation form (see Chapter 7).

INITIATE THE INSTRUCTION

1. Don't call you instruction "library instruction." Begin calling it information literacy instruction. Few teachers and students care about what you want to accomplish for the library, but many will care a lot about information literacy as it applies directly to their curriculum, in the classroom, or throughout the school.

2. Examine the curriculum guide; think about specific classes and assignments for each grade where information literacy is a good fit.

3. Approach teachers with whom you already have a working relationship and who use your library regularly. Offer them the first opportunities for your new instruction and promise that they will see better results with their students concerning the class research and assignments as a result of the instruction. Don't worry—there will be better results. If you don't have any regulars or teachers with whom you work well, question why not and change what is necessary to fix the problem.

4. Figure out who holds the decision-making power (or political power) with regard to your school's curriculum and work closely with that person (or those people) to find out how to make certain every student at every grade level will

be reached for information literacy instruction. Even if you already know the answer, the confirmation that you will need to reach each student at each grade level will give you leverage for approaching teachers who might be initially reluctant to give up class time. Ask for input about which classes might be the most advantageous, and approach those teachers with the good news that the principal or academic dean recommended their classes. Combine this with whatever rationale or reward you can think of to sweeten the offer and motivate the teacher to jump on board.

Use your knowledge of available resources to make connections to specific assignments and projects for teachers who may not have time to investigate the latest titles and materials for the topic. Offer to jump-start an assignment and project for those teachers and to focus specifically on what they want students to learn. Create challenges and search strategies that target the class assignment directly. The teacher's reward is that you are doing the research preparation for them and ensuring that students will be successful in finding appropriate information for their assignments.

You will undoubtedly spend a lot of time doing preliminary research so that the strategies presented during instruction will reinforce what you are teaching them instead of demonstrating the "wrong" way with precious moments ticking away. Of course, things are more likely to go wrong when you've got a class in front of you, so don't expect perfection; use the "oops" moments to demonstrate your sense of humor and how everyone can learn from their mistakes. In addition, always remind students that research is a series of trials and errors and that you learn just as much from the mistakes as you do from the successes.

IMPROVE AND ADAPT YOUR INSTRUCTION

Work constantly to provide flexibility for schedule changes, to accomodate teacher requests and to accomodate needs, and to find out what's new in popular culture. Commit to engaging your students by the themes and topics of popular culture. Never is a plan—even a plan supported and approved by administration—enough to bring instruction to life and keep it alive. When you get bored with your instruction, chances are the students were bored yesterday or last week.

KEEPING THE BUY-IN

Despite the hard work involved, a new and exciting program is sometimes easier to start than to keep going. Teachers are eager to see what you have, students have picked up on the buzz about library games, and administration has given you pats on the back and recognition. But what happens when it's not as much fun as it was last year? What happens when teachers aren't quite as eager to schedule with you? With luck, you'll tweak your program and come up with fresh new ideas before that happens. And with the publicity tips in Chapter 9 together with your commitment to staying tuned in to the newest fads and trends in pop culture, you'll keep your instruction and library program fresh for you own sake as well as for the sake of the students.

A SCHOOLWIDE INFORMATION LITERACY MODEL

By the time your school is benefiting from your information literacy instruction, project and assignment pages, and your role as a leader in developing information literate students, it will be necessary to consider making information literacy a schoolwide effort. A schoolwide standard with consistent expectations and means of assessing information literacy and research needs to be understood, accepted, and integrated into every classroom and learning opportunity in your school for students to be provided with the reinforcement they need.

In most cases, this means that the teachers must receive training regarding information literacy. All educators must begin with the same definition, with a common vocabulary, understanding, and expectation of achieving information literacy, before they can be expected to become its prophets.

What your information literacy and research model should include is a step-by-step guide that moves a student from examining the question or task that an assignment poses through the additional steps to completing and evaluating the assignment or project. The expectation is that this process of evaluation, analysis, and critical thinking will become intuitive when students have reinforcement through repeated experiences with the process.

CREATING A SCHOOLWIDE MODEL

It is likely that you already have some knowledge about research and information literacy models if you've participated in any library conferences, conventions, or workshops or read any professional journals in the past few years. The concept isn't new, but getting an entire school to participate and support the effort is somewhat unusual. It takes administrative support and participation to promote the initiative, but it takes every single educator to keep it going. Take a look at the sample in Chapter 8 that individualizes and adapts a model for a specific school.

It is necessary to make your individual research model as attractive and engaging as possible to have teachers and students find it relevant. Examine popular research models such as The Big6 (http://www.big6.com) and the Research Cycle (http://questioning.org/Q6/research.html) and compare them with your school's needs and standards. Then adapt them or elements of them or create an individualized model for your school. The following steps will help you get started:

1. Based on your Graded Course of Study, locate skills and goals that need reinforcement for every grade level.

2. Determine a strategy for moving from the beginning to the end of any project.

3. Integrate critical-thinking and inquiry-based learning skills into appropriate steps.

4. Select the number of steps that best fits your school. Be careful not to have so many that it becomes intimidating or so few that each step is too broad.

Find a way to make the steps easy to remember. Create an acronym that's meaningful for your school (see Chapter 6 for an example).

PRESENT THE PLAN

1. Gain approval from the administration and decision makers in your school.

2. After gaining approval, present a workshop or have a meeting to inform and demonstrate for all department chairs and teachers who participate in curriculum decisions how beneficial a schoolwide effort will be in developing information-literate students. Describe your plan for bringing teachers on board and how and when you expect to begin the implementation stage. Offer supporting evidence and research that concerns the information literacy and research model as a schoolwide standard.

3. Present the model to all teachers and educators, with supporting evidence and research, and respond to questions and feedback.

4. Determine needs for teacher in-service or workshops with regard to the plan.

INITIATE THE MODEL AND PLAN

1. Set a timeline for implementation of the plan.

2. Initiate the information literacy and research model in your school.

IMPROVE AND ADAPT YOUR MODEL

1. Seek feedback concerning the model.

2. Improve and adapt the model as needed.

REFERENCES

American Library Association. (1998a). *Information Power: Building Partnerships for Learning* (2nd ed.). Chicago: Author.

American Library Association. (1998b). *Information Literacy Standards for Student Learning*. American Library Association. Chicago: Author.

Chapter 6

Life in the Real World

THE STUDENTS ARE IN YOUR LIBRARY. NOW WHAT DO YOU DO WITH THEM?

You've got the buy-in from administrators and teachers, a class of students scheduled in the library next week, but the graded course of study next to your computer isn't offering inspiration and enlightenment for the blank PowerPoint presentation blinking at you from your computer screen. Take a look at this chapter and glean some ideas for your own school and learn from these personal experiences.

THE REAL WORLD

Using the following graded course of study from my own school, Figure 6.1 shows the plan that launched the instruction at my school with the intention of making certain that every student at every grade level made some gains toward information literacy and research skills.

GRADED COURSE OF STUDY

Library Department

PHILOSOPHY

The St. Ursula Library provides atmosphere, resources, leadership, and instruction that will allow students to become sophisticated information and knowledge managers. Each student is challenged to think logically, critically, and discriminately with the expectation of becoming leaders and lifelong learners. The Library anticipates and plans support for curriculum, along with the personal interests and professional needs of students and faculty in order to make certain that students become information literate before graduating.

GENERAL INSTRUCTIONAL OBJECTIVES

The St. Ursula Academy Library exists to serve as the school's information center. The Library's program includes consultation, instruction, and leadership, in its role of providing intellectual accesses to information. With respect for traditional roles and collections, the program and its facility embraces an electronic environment, and maintains a flexible, adaptable, and expandable vision in order to meet the changing needs of its role in the 21st century.

SPECIFIC INSTRUCTIONAL GOALS AND OBJECTIVES

Freshman Year

Goal—Students show examples of fact finding to resolve an information problem or question

Levels of knowledge required:

- Understanding the differences among library tools and why one would be chosen over another
- Showing examples of credible information vs. biased or misinformation
- Using the electronic card catalog to locate materials
- Knowing how to locate items from a result list in the card catalog
- Demonstrating basic searching skills—electronic resources and WWW
- Evaluating information
- Avoiding plagiarism
- Knowing that there is a world of research beyond fact finding

Sophomore Year

Goal—Students demonstrate examples of critical thinking skills that go beyond fact finding to resolve an information problem or question.

Levels of knowledge required:

- Demonstrating the differences between accurate and inaccurate information and complete and incomplete information for a specific task
- Using both broad and specific questions that will help in finding information
- Using the card catalog with a greater level of skill and understanding how subject, keyword, and author searches will reap different results
- Understanding that a range of sources of information might meet an information need

- Understanding the differences among the various electronic resources at SUA and other libraries
- Evaluating information
- Developing and using successful strategies for locating information
- Using Boolean logic and punctuation in a search strategy
- Determining which resources are more likely to satisfy need
- Understanding Plagiarism and copyright
- Assimilating information into a project or assignment

Junior Year

Goal—Students understand that there is information on more than one side of an issue and remain open to other perspectives; they also judge the completeness of their information before making a decision.

Levels of knowledge required:

- Formulating and revising plans for accessing information for a range of needs and situations
- Understanding and using most appropriate resources available
- Using a full range of information sources to meet differing information needs
- Understanding of resources at SUA and other libraries and information sources
- Understanding process of utilizing the Greater Cincinnati Library Consoratium resources
- Revising, adding, and deleting questions as information needs change
- Demonstrating ability to perform sophisticated search strategies in the card catalog, electronic resources, and on the WWW
- Judging the quality, accuracy, and completeness of the information retrieved
- Assimilating the information into the research paper
- Understanding plagiarism and copyright

Senior Year

Goal—Students quickly and effectively locate the most relevant information for research questions within the sources they have gathered, and they vary their strategies according to the format, organization, and search capability of the sources and according to the particular issue they are researching.

- Students apply sophisticated information-seeking skills and assimilation of information into decision making
- Students are able to expand their research beyond St. Ursula's Academy to other libraries and information sources
- Students are prepared to apply learned skills to college and beyond

Reference

American Library Association. *Information Power: Building Partnerships for Learning.* Chicago: American Library Association, 1998.

Figure 6.1. Sample Graded Course of Study.

REACH EVERY STUDENT

The grade levels and the required subject or class in Figure 6.2 are the results of the effort to find classes that were required for each grade level. By senior year, most students have completed their required classes (although some seniors occasionally end up in junior, sophomore, and freshmen classes) so I do not target a single class for seniors and instead use classes for which teachers request information and research instruction.

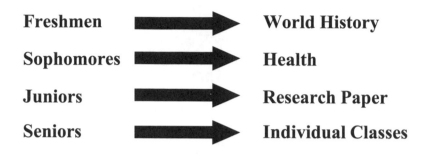

Freshmen ⟶ **World History**

Sophomores ⟶ **Health**

Juniors ⟶ **Research Paper**

Seniors ⟶ **Individual Classes**

Figure 6.2. Grade levels and the targeted subject.

Freshmen

Every freshman takes world history, and the *Survivor* or *The Amazing Race* games are used for their information literacy and research skills instruction.

As I said before, the instruction changes constantly. This adventure began with asking teachers for three 90-minute classes. Teachers agreed, and for a year and a half those 270 minutes were used with every class each term. Because of a block schedule with a four-bell day, this meant that for most classes, instruction with new classes occurred every quarter, which kept us very busy for the first few weeks of each term (and limited other students and classes who wanted library time). Halfway through the second year, however, after a couple of single-session lessons due to sudden scheduling changes or teacher requests, it became obvious that some elements of the instruction could be cut with similar good results. We removed a few challenges that were redundant (yet provided more practice and review), and because teachers were teaching students how to create bibliographies, we left that to them. We also slimmed down the instruction about the Internet and search engines because we covered the warnings and search strategies by comparing and contrasting information found on the Web and in proprietary databases during the databases and scholarly information lessons. Things ran more efficiently and quickly, and students were still learning what they needed. Teachers were pleased to have the class time back, and students seemed happy to get on with their assignment—they seemed to value the time more because they knew that this was their best shot at getting help with their assignment.

Freshmen are ideal for the *Survivor* or *Amazing Race* games because we combine a library orientation with the information literacy instruction. The fun and lighthearted approach to research, information, and the library make a positive first impression on freshmen and demonstrate that the library is an enjoyable place to be. With library hours from 7:30 A.M. to 5:00 P.M. daily, the library is often a retreat for freshmen because their rides are dependent on bus, parent, and carpool schedules. We remind them that they can complete their homework before their sports practice or game by coming to the library after school.

Sophomores

Sophomores experience a completely different format. We use four or five entire class sessions that relate directly to their daily class topics to immerse them in the library and the information that they are seeking. The instruction is subtle, and they don't seem to notice that they are being instructed in research skills and information literacy. Here are the five components to the sophomore sessions:

1. Early in the term, sophomore health classes come to the library with topics in hand and instructions from their teacher to check out nonfiction books on their health topics. Before they head to the stacks and library catalog, there is a discussion about how many views can be presented about a single topic and how a well-balanced library should provide all the various views on a topic. We also bring in popular culture with examples from TV shows, movies, and the media that present biased views about topics. For example, teens having sexual relationships in movies—does that encourage or discourage teens' sexual activity? Or how is teen violence (such as the Columbine High School or Minnesota's Red Lake Indian Reservation shootings) portrayed in the media? Is the information biased, exaggerated, or accurate? We challenge students to locate material that would demonstrate their personal view on a topic from the library catalog. When they do, they are asked to locate information with another viewpoint. Their assignment is to learn about differing viewpoints of a single issue and to present them in an essay that the teacher assigns. Many students are amazed that there are so many opinions about drug use and legalization, gun control, parental rights, eating disorders, treatments for various illnesses, and so forth. In addition, we discuss the importance of locating the most current information for health-related topics as well as technology, science, and other issues. By the time they complete this instruction, students understand how books are published and why, who the authors and editors might be, how there might not be a single correct answer to a difficult topic, how information is biased, that there is a huge difference among information sources, and that a review of efficient and thorough searching of the library catalog is necessary. Emphasis on avoiding plagiarism is presented with this class, and finally the students leave the library with a book in hand and are reminded how easily they can take portable information home with them that doesn't require cables, electricity, or bandwidth.

2. The second session consists of using three research databases to locate consumer health information about smoking. The session begins with narrowing general topics of smoking and teens. With our prompting, students work to make the topics very specific and relevant to their lives; we encourage them to think about advertisements, television, movies, and other information sources that make them aware of smoking topics. They then begin creating search strategies using Boolean logic, truncation, and punctuation; they make decisions about searching using keyword, subject, or browsing for topics. After reviewing what they've learned as freshmen and practiced to this point, they move on to the higher-level task of comparing and contrasting two valuable sources of information. Students are expected to understand the differences among scholarly works, primary and secondary sources, which databases are best for this specific assignment, and how to assimilate the information into their project. The project

they complete is a simple essay assigned by their teacher that compares three articles on their topic. Even though the essay is not a formal research paper, the steps they take to complete the essay involve critical thinking and logic, and, we hope, urge them to look at their world and how information is presented to them in a different and more analytical way.

3. The third session is a favorite with sophomores. Students come to the library as a class with the task of locating a book of fiction, nonfiction written as a reflection or memoir, or a biography or autobiography that relates to any health issue (we constantly praise the teacher for incorporating literature into her or his subject). Students aren't told until they arrive that book talks are planned for the day and that they can sit back, relax, and listen to some novels. It's important to spend some time choosing books that will be certain to interest them and bookmark pages that will peak their curiosity and motivate them to want to read the entire book. The stress of their days will visibly fall from their shoulders as you begin with the synopsis of the book and then read from a chapter or two. As the final book is completed, allow them to share books that they love and recommend them to each other. Offer the books that you've just read to them for check out, and then move on to the electronic catalog and the stacks for browsing and locating the books that others need. Remind them how best to search the catalog, and you'll be sliding in a review of research skills without them even noticing it. The students have several weeks to read their book and to write an essay that the teacher assigns about the book. Students often return their books early and ask for more suggestions.

4. The fourth session with sophomores involves locating consumer health information on the Web. When asking the class where they first go to locate information about a sports injury or health issue, undoubtedly the unanimous chant "Google" vibrates through the library. We follow up by asking them how they determine whether the information is provided by a health professional or some guy without any health or medical education whose only intention is to make money attracting advertisement to his Web site. Continuing with the discussion about why it's important to know who and what organization is responsible for information on the site, we remind them to complete an Internet site evaluation form (see Chapter 7) for every Web site they use in their assignment if they use Google or any other search engine. Tips on how to save time and effort by finding credible sites that don't require them to fill out the evaluation form are offered. We then demonstrate, and have them demonstrate, how to search the library catalog for Web sites, locate them through proprietary databases, and by using the project and assignment pages (see Chapter 8) that have been created in collaboration with teachers. We explain to them that these sites are reviewed, evaluated, and deemed credible and useful, so there is no reason to evaluate them again. We remind them, however, that they still need to determine the site's worth and value as it applies to their specific need. Finally, we ask if they are convinced that it's more efficient to search credible resources that we have acquired specifically for high school student school curriculum from the beginning. If they aren't convinced, we ask for a volunteer to demonstrate and compare results of an Internet search engine search and one through our electronic catalog or proprietary database.

5. The final session with sophomores occurs during exams. Students come to the library for both a review and for assessment, but instead of the traditional methods of assessments, we reward them with the end-of-term game, "Who Wants to Be an Infoaire?" (see Chapter 8) based loosely on the television game show, *Who Wants to Be a Millionaire?* Students break up into teams, and the teams earn points by participating in and demonstrating the knowledge they've gained over the term. Topics that relate to the health class include wellness, nutrition, first aid, alcohol and drugs, tobacco, illness, and relationships. The questions and challenges built into the game require knowledge about the best resources for locating specific health-related information, the strategies for searching the resources, and finally some analysis and evaluation of the information they find. The teacher can be involved as the scorekeeper if she or he wants to provide grades for the teams or individuals.

Juniors

Junior year seems to be the year when things begin to click with most students. They no longer have to think about where to find our library catalog and materials. They've used fairly sophisticated search strategies for more than two years, and their critical-thinking skills and common sense are maturing. As you know, all schools change, and our school is making a transition from a required junior research paper class to the integration of a research paper into a literature class, and the process of changing instruction to suit the new assignment is underway. Unfortunately, the research paper class was perfect for information literacy instruction because students were able to choose their own topic, and they were very enthusiastic about finding information that proved their thesis and personal opinion. With the research paper classes, we would ask students to describe their topics and interests and give them the task of narrowing or broadening them, creating search strategies, and discussing how many ways they could approach the topic to make their final projects interesting (they also do a PowerPoint presentation in class that summarizes their paper). They were also required to use various types of resources as well, which was a natural fit for instruction at their level.

Well, the best laid plans. . . . The research paper is now a literary criticism paper, and the buy-in from students that existed with personally selected topics, as well as the connection to their real world through current culture and news topics, is not quite as strong. It is, however, an easier instruction to prepare, present, and have understood by the students because they don't move beyond literary resources. The difference between scholarly literary criticism and the information they find through Internet search engines is vast and becomes quickly obvious to them as well. The plus side is that they do get to delve into very sophisticated, college-level information searching and gathering methods, and the students quickly move toward independence in understanding when and where to select specific sources (at least for literary criticism). Although students do search beyond the school's catalog in earlier years, juniors are expected to utilize more college-level databases to locate scholarly journal articles and information. Although freshmen and sophomores are reminded that we belong to the Greater Cincinnati Library Consortium (GCLC), which means that they can borrow materials and use electronic resources from most libraries in the city and beyond, the juniors actually begin to venture out to the academic and special libraries. It's exciting to watch them gain confidence and the ability to research beyond our walls and to use the databases and catalogs that they will be using in college in a few years.

Discussing plagiarism and copyright and what that means to our society and to them as individuals reinforces the ethical use of technology and information. The opportunity is most useful for reminding them how all aspiring writers, musicians, and artists should be concerned with copyright laws because those who illegally download music or make illegal copies of books or articles deny the creator the royalties that will allow them to continue to create works and pursue a career of their choice. Students begin to understand how copyright benefits society rather than existing only to complicate their research papers and assignments.

Seniors

We expect seniors to pull all the information literacy and research skills together in their final year. By now they should be able to gather a wide variety of information independently and determine its academic value. Because most seniors are working on electives and very few move together through classes, there are fewer opportunities for formal instruction for seniors only. Some seniors end up completing required classes with freshmen, sophomores, and juniors because those classes didn't fit into their schedules at the normal time. This allows them to receive the benefits of review and reinforcement of skills they've learned in earlier years. We provide research overviews for any willing classes at any grade level to remind them which resources might be most useful, and we offer constant one-on-one with seniors as well as other students.

CHANGING TIMES

Even as this book is being written, our academic dean is suggesting changes for freshmen and sophomore requirements. Perhaps the health class will move down to freshmen level and the choice between using health or world history for freshmen instruction will need to be made. Then we'll also need to find a common class for sophomores. I constantly worry that the teachers whom I work with best will retire or leave our school and that our instruction may be weakened. However, despite my worry, the changes are ultimately positive because they give us the opportunity to revise, change, and adapt the instruction constantly to what's happening with our students.

The best scenario occurs when a teacher comes to you for collaboration in creating an assignment or lesson. It would be wonderful if there were a strategy that's sure to work and couldn't fail, but it usually comes down to plain stubbornness and tenacity that will see the plan through to success. That determination to see the plan through is up to all of us individually. Without campaigning, making suggestions, becoming part of the decision-making team of the school, all library programs will slide into mediocrity. We have to maintain a level of energy that surpasses the energy level of all other school faculty, staff, and administration to make our library program successful.

Chapter 7

What They Need to Know

COVERING THE ESSENTIALS

We've looked at methods of integrating your school's standards or graded course of study into a working instructional plan that reaches all students in your school in a meaningful way. Pop culture is the hook for keeping your students tuned in, but it's the essential elements of your instruction that will help them become information literate.

Your standards and Graded Course of Study are written in black and white, but unfortunately, in the real world, things are not quite as simple. We use our plans to keep us on track, but with schedule and class changes, teacher assignment changes, and unexpected interruptions, we can't count on things being the same one day to the next. Take the time you have and cover the essential elements of your information literacy plan in an engaging way. Think of each element as a building block that students will use to gain more and more proficiency and knowledge throughout their education and their lives. Help them discover and understand the progression from information to knowledge to wisdom. Create a skills level chart to keep you on track and to use as a basis for a checklist for covering the skills and knowledge that you determine to be essential. Take a look at the skills chart in Figure 7.1.

Information Literacy and Research Skills

Freshman Year (World History and American Citizenship)

Levels of knowledge required:

- ❏ Understanding the differences among library tools and why one would be chosen over another
- ❏ Showing examples of credible information versus biased or misinformation
- ❏ Using the electronic catalog to locate materials
- ❏ Knowing how to locate items from result list in the card catalog
- ❏ Demonstrating basic searching skills—electronic resources and Internet
- ❏ Evaluating information
- ❏ Avoiding plagiarism
- ❏ Knowing that there is a world of research beyond fact finding

Sophomore Year (Health)

Levels of knowledge required:

- ❏ Demonstrating the differences between accurate and inaccurate information and complete and incomplete information for a specific task
- ❏ Using both broad and specific questions that will help in finding information
  - Using the electronic catalog with a greater level of skill and understanding how subject, keyword, and author searches will reap different results
- ❏ Understanding that a range of sources of information might meet an information need
  - Understanding the differences among the various electronic resources at St. Ursula's Academy (SUA) and other libraries
  - Evaluating information
- ❏ Developing and using successful strategies for locating information
  - Using Boolean logic and punctuation in a search strategy
  - Determining which resources are more likely to satisfy need
- ❏ Understanding plagiarism and copyright
- ❏ Assimilating information into a project or assignment

Junior Year (Literary Criticism)

Levels of knowledge required:

- ❑ Formulating and revising plans for accessing information for a range of needs and situations
    - Understanding and using most appropriate resources available
- ❑ Using a full range of information sources to meet differing information needs
    - Understanding of resources at SUA and other libraries and information sources
    - Understanding process of utilizing the Greater Cincinnati Library Consortium resources
- ❑ Revising, adding, and deleting questions as information needs change
    - Demonstrating ability to perform sophisticated search strategies in the card catalog, electronic resources, and on the Internet
- ❑ Judging the quality, accuracy, and completeness of the information retrieved
- ❑ Assimilating the information into the literacy criticism paper
- ❑ Understanding plagiarism and copyright

Senior Year (Various Classes)

Levels of knowledge required:

- ❑ Students apply sophisticated information-seeking skills and assimilation of information into decision making
- ❑ Students are able to expand their research beyond SUA to other libraries and information sources
- ❑ Students are prepared to apply learned skills to college and beyond

Figure 7.1. Information literacy goals year by year.

From *Using Pop Culture to Teach Information Literacy: Methods to Engage a New Generation* by Linda D. Behen. Westport, CT: Libraries Unlimited. Copyright © 2006.

LIGHTEN UP

We take what we do very seriously, and we always aim for the best. But we don't want students to learn the essentials of information literacy in a rote and academic way that doesn't transfer from the classroom to their daily life. For example, rather than have students be able to recite the steps for evaluating a Web site, encourage them to question and analyze what might be the purpose or intention of a specific Web site. It may be the few things they remember from your sophomore instruction about opposing or biased viewpoints that encourage them to question and analyze the next billboard, movie trailer, or article they see about the topics of pollution, bioethics, or family relations. So what if they can't fully name the terms used for scholarly material (peer reviewed, refereed, etc.) as long as they know the differences between the writings of a journalist and an expert in a specific field?

WHAT EVERY STUDENT MUST KNOW BY COLLEGE

There are elements of information literacy that students can't afford to lack at graduation. Without these skills and knowledge that give them flexibility, confidence, and independence in finding useful information for both academic and personal purposes, transition from high school to college will be most difficult. Keep in mind that your graduate is someone else's first-year student who will take an attitude and impression of libraries and information with them to college and beyond. It's our job to make it a positive attitude and impression and to send them off with a full toolbox of skills that apply to any information-seeking situation. The most useful elements of information literacy are universal and can be transferred to a multitude of situations, and they almost always overlap. For example, given that students already know what makes scholarly material reliable and credible and that scholarly resources are usually limited through subscription databases that are password protected, it's the elements of publishing and copyright, security, and proprietary permissions that are the essential piece that students need to know and understand. By the time they graduate from high school, students must know why it isn't likely that they can find a literary criticism in a reputable scholarly journal about *Leaves of Grass* through a Web search engine and why all the "good stuff" is usually secured and limited to patrons of a specific school, university, or public library system. Although you can relate to students' frustration in not being able to "Google" their way through research, the gained knowledge that allows them to recognize the value of "good" information will introduce copyright and publishing issues, and the difference between scholarly and general information that will see them through the rest of their lives.

No matter how many steps your information literacy standards and models have, the essential breakdown of steps naturally falls into three categories: defining the information need, selecting and accessing information sources, and evaluating information sources.

Start defining these categories to your students, and you'll see eyes rolling, yawns, and "who cares" glares. Fear not. Just as everything necessary falls into these categories, so, too, do these categories fall into the other categories in which students can immediately relate. Students want to solve their pressing information needs with as little effort as possible. By engaging them through pop culture themes, we teach students to define the information need, select and access information sources, and evaluate their information sources with them hardly noticing. When your school adopts a schoolwide information literacy model, the steps described here will become so familiar to them after years of repetition and reinforcement that the pieces will become intuitive; they will automatically begin to evaluate and analyze their information needs from start to finish. But as we struggle to adopt that schoolwide information literacy model with complete buy-in from teachers and administration and move our students to the level where they become wise information users, we need to plug away with the time and essential tools available to us.

The categories of defining the information need, selecting and accessing information sources, and evaluating information sources can be taught to students thoroughly through the tools that they use daily in school and at home. All essential skills and information fall into the following categories, and you will know that you have made steps toward developing information-savvy students when you see them applying the specific knowledge to new and different tasks:

- Publishing Basics

- Technology and Media

- Research Skills

It's difficult to imagine that a student can successfully complete any assignment in today's classroom without using computers, computer software, the Internet, and media tools to assimilate credible and useful information efficiently into a video, a PowerPoint presentation, or a word-processed document. Imagine going through life without the skills to evaluate and select useful information for personal, academic, or professional purpose. Let's take a look at these categories with the essential skills and tools that fall within each one.

PUBLISHING BASICS

Discussion about publishing usually begins with an information need for a specific research task or assignment. Students benefit from understanding how types of information differ and how they can more quickly determine how to make choices about what they need. Students know that information comes in print books, journal and magazine articles, electronic databases, on Web pages, or on DVDs or CD-ROMs. Do they understand why a publisher is willing to spend tens of thousands of dollars to publish and market a single book, why an author might choose to write a ten- or twenty-page article instead of writing a book, or why a student might choose the format of a DVD over a print book? Do they know that people such as librarians, teachers, experts, friends, family, and authors are information sources as well and that speeches, interviews, documents, and statements can be some of the most valuable types of information? Have they ever heard the term "Publish or Perish"? How do all of the aspects affect their information choices and needs?

Raising these questions allows the opportunity to share knowledge about the intent of copyright, the publishing process, and the diversity of information. It enables you to help students analyze a scholarly article in *Shakespeare's Quarterly* versus an article about Shakespeare in *Newsweek*, why a primary source offers an opportunity for original thought and theories, and how information from an encyclopedia, a book, or a magazine differs greatly and yet how each can serve an important purpose in research.

Tell students the price of expensive reference sets and scholarly books. Give them the cost for an annual subscription to a single database and explain the steps you took in determining to choose it over a similar one. Walk them through the levels of development and evaluation involved in the creation of a database, book, or article. Explain how the database development process begins with individual pieces of information such as a journal article or book and how the individual information sources are either peer reviewed or chosen by editors to appear in a publication. Continue with the process of how the publication is selected for inclusion in a database based on state and national curriculum standards, socially and academically accepted and recognized excellence, and relevance to a student population. Describe how focus groups, beta users, and reviewers spend a lot of time testing and making recommendations for improvement before the database is sold to customers. Define the never-ending marketing efforts and how reviews by library gods and goddesses in library journals are written to recommend a resource. Finally, tell your students how you use their frustrations, successes, and daily results to determine annually whether to keep a database or replace it with another. At this point, they should be convinced that the review process is never ending.

Don't forget to include the author's perspective in your discussion so that students understand who writes, why they write, and the intention of their published works. Ask students if they know who might write an article about a Roman god in *Journal of Contemporary Religion* and who writes a story in *Time* about the same topic. Ask them about both authors' possible education and purpose for writing, along with the intended audience, and give an example of an appropriate need for both. Discuss the current news stories about both academic experts and journalists who have plagiarized or fabricated information in their published works and how shortcuts can be fatal to a career and to personal credibility. Ask them how that might affect their own assignments if they had used these as sources. Segue into the copyright issue by imagining how empty library shelves would be if authors couldn't make a living by writing books. Describe how artists and writers often depend on the income from their works to make a living and to have time and incentive to create. Ask students to consider how empty bookstores, libraries, and museums might be if authors and artists had to choose other careers to earn a paycheck. Wonder out loud how the piracy of music and movies affect the music and movie industry. Ask them if they would ever walk into a music or movie store and steal an album or movie, and ask them how buying, copying, or downloading on the black market differs. Hopefully, students will see the similarity and begin to understand that copyright serves a useful purpose to society and that they may one day be the artist, writer, or musician whose livelihood depends on the income from the sale of their product.

Delivery Methods

Describe how magazine and journal articles differ only in the delivery method for articles found in a print journal or through a database (you might need to convince some teachers of that as well). Physically hold up a *Smithsonian* issue and turn to an article. Locate an electronic version of the same article and demonstrate how the two articles are exactly the same. Explain the difference between a PDF file and an HTML file and how the information in a PDF file is an image of the original article and can't be manipulated or changed. Warn them that the PDF version might be required for research sources by their future professors or in graduate school for exactly that reason. Finally, wonder out loud how a new type of file or technology may replace the PDF format in the future.

Students don't usually give much thought to timeliness with relationship to information. They are very inconsistent in what they consider current or old. They may consider all information from ten years ago to be ancient and disregard it for their history or literature research. On the other hand, they may not understand how important the most current information for health, science, or technology needs is and that three years is considered archaic for some topics. Explain how long it takes to research, write, find a publisher, edit, print, and market a book and how expensive the process can be for both an author and publisher. Tell them that a book about technology may already be two years old by the time it hits the library shelf. Describe how the most current information on any topic is usually found in an article because it takes authors less time to research and write the shorter work and that the periodicals are published at a regular interval that allows for fairly timely publishing. Remind students that timeliness isn't the only quality to consider; often a more comprehensive view of an issue is needed. Discuss how professors' careers usually depend on researching and publishing in their field and how publishing in peer-reviewed, refereed, and scholarly works are required for them to be promoted and achieve longevity at an institution. Take the opportunity to discuss who the intended audience is for these works and the decision-making process about using any information for academic or personal needs. Hopefully, the publishing background that you provide will have an impact on student's current and future relationship with information.

Bibliographies

Students often have "ah-ha" moments when they are citing and creating bibliographies that clarify the differences between scholarly and general information, Web pages and journal articles, reference information, and books (or ebooks) that live on the Internet. Although students usually consider bibliographies to be a torture device, we (teachers and library gods and goddesses) should hold them to the rigors of accurate citing. In many ways, creating bibliographies can be compared to the sentence diagramming of the past that helped to organize and categorize information for us. Teach your students to approach online templates and citation-making software with caution because of occasional errors that are found. Certainly many online bibliographic tools are accurate, but you can use the opportunity to reinforce how they need to always question and evaluate all information even if the origin is a university or reputable organization or vendor.

TECHNOLOGY AND MEDIA

Providing students with opportunities to develop flexible attitudes toward technology and media will ease the transition to newer and different technological tools that they will be certain to meet in the future. We take for granted that students will enter high school with the basic knowledge of using computers and the Internet. Few freshmen (although it seems there are always a few) will need to be taught how to log in to a computer and to find the available Web browser and software programs. But they will all need to be taught the specifics of your school's network. For example, incoming students will need a username and password to initially log in, knowledge about saving materials to a network drive and information on the school's technology policies and rules, and how to access their e-mail and programs from home. If your school and library provides remote access (and it should), students will need usernames and passwords to enter databases and files from remote locations. And there is always the transition for some students going from one operating system to another. It's always a good idea to provide a generic student login for students who forget their password or who aren't able to log in successfully for whatever reason so that valuable research or instruction time isn't lost. They can still participate in the instruction and fix their problem later.

Although this seems to fall into simple facts and instructions instead of information literacy skills, the value lies in learning that in college, at work, and in any future organizations to which they belong, there will be the same transition period involved with new ways of doing things. It's a good reminder to students to stay flexible when working with technology because it's rarely going to be the way it was the last time. As with other information, if someone else at your school teaches these basics, you don't need to duplicate efforts; however, these are things students need to know, and it does fit easily into information literacy instruction.

Just as access to operating systems and networks vary and change, so do the information sources that students use. Perhaps a favorite magazine database is no longer available or you've chosen to replace it with another. Once students become aware of the change and they know that the information they need can be located in a different resource, they will be able to transfer all their skills and knowledge fairly quickly to the new database by applying the critical-thinking skills they've been developing. Point out that all databases utilize the same methods of retrieving information and that browsing, search strategies using punctuation and Boolean logic, subject searching, an so on will always result in the best results. The more experience students have using different interfaces in individual databases, the better prepared they will be to search the next new database that they meet. One word of caution: don't make searching too easy. High school libraries that choose to use software that incorporates all the information sources, Web sites, and databases into a single search interface may be doing their students a disservice. Sure, they'll easily locate what they need with a single search (perhaps), but will they develop the flexibility and experience to apply their knowledge and skills to new situations and sources?

Are there any students in your high school who would admit to not knowing everything they need to know about the Web? Not likely. Most can't remember when there wasn't an Internet or Web, and they've been "Asking Jeeves" or "Googling" for information since they were in primary school. It can be difficult, but not impossible, to break their bad habits. The essential elements that they need to understand about the Internet to become sophisticated information consumers follow.

Web Sites

Everybody and anybody can create and post a Web site for any topic or purpose. Some individuals' sole purpose in creating Web pages appears to be in drawing advertisers to make money. Explain to students how most advertisers are interested in sites that draw high numbers of hits and that some advertisers only care about the numbers of times a site is visited rather than the value of information posted. Students become very interested in hearing that advertisers may not even know what information the site includes. Describe to students how you could sit down right now and create a Web site for the prevention of diabetes and post it on the Web in the next few hours. Explain how you could simply copy and paste information from other sites, journal articles (scholarly or not), adding the little you might know about diabetes yourself. Warn that your lack of training as a physician or expert in the medical field or in the study of diabetes would prevent any cohesive or accurate presentation of the assembled information. Tell them that some of the information might be perfectly fine (depending on the sources you copied), but some may be dangerously flawed because of your inability to know the difference. Point out that someone with diabetes who is not information literate and who doesn't know how to evaluate the information may read and use the information and experience harmful results.

Hopefully, students will begin to understand that inaccurate information may not only result in a poor grade, but that it can be dangerous to them or their loved ones. Point out how health consumers can avoid risky information by relying on sources in reputable databases, scholarly information, or from national organizations recommended by their physicians or health care providers. This discussion is a good segue into evaluating Web sites and how they can avoid misinformation by choosing sources that you or their teachers (or that are part of a proven subscription database) have recommended for research. Define the elements of Web site evaluation and walk through a Web site evaluation form (Figure 7.2).

Ask students if they are familiar with the different terms related to Web sites. Ask them to define a URL (uniform access locator), the extension of the URL, and so on. Ask how they can look at the extensions (.org, .com, .edu, etc.) and begin to evaluate a Web site based on the extension. Most will know that .edu represents education, and some will know that it is college or university level, but when asked, most will assume that an .edu site is automatically credible because a university's purpose is to educate. Pushing them a little further, ask them about the personal homepages that students create using their university's server that have the .edu extension. Suggest the following scenario: a freshmen college student in her first semester studying Shakespeare gets a "C" on her essay. She thinks her paper is worthy of an "A," and she wants the world to see it and recognize it as a great work. So she posts it on her personal university Web page. Ask them what will happen if they use that essay as a resource for their own Shakespeare assignment. It's not likely they will get better than a "C," and it's very likely that they'll earn less than a "C" once that information is watered down another level and their teacher questions the credibility of the source.

Reinforce how important it is to understand who the author is and what his or her credentials are despite what the extension is or with which institution the author is affiliated. Remind them that there are no Internet police who cruise the Web for bad or misleading information. Warn them to discard any sites that don't give them author information and to move on to information that does for the sake of efficiency and quality.

Make certain that students understand that proprietary databases are not Web pages and explain that databases only live on the Web to be accessible from remote locations and various operating systems.

WWW Site Evaluation Form

1. How did you locate this Web site?

    a. Library Catalog _____

    b. Search engine_____ which One?_____

    c. Other_____

2. What is the URL? _____

    a. What's the extension?_____

    b. Does the extension indicate that the site might be credible?_____

    c. Why? Why Not?_____

3. Does the site load quickly?_____

4. Is the information you're seeking clearly displayed on the first page of the site?

_____

    a. Is there an internal search engine for locating your topic quickly?_____

    b. Do you have to guess where to go to locate your topic?_____
    Explain_____

    c. How much time did it take you to locate your topic?_____

5. Who is the author or the person(s) responsible for this Web site?

_____

6. How do you know whether the author is credible?

_____

7. How current is the information?_____ Is a date given that indicates an
update?_____What is it?_____

8. What's the purpose of the information? To sell? To inform? To persuade? How do
you know?
Explain_____

9. Are you choosing this site to use for your assignment? _____

    a. Why is the information worthwhile? _____

    b. How does it solve your research need?_____

Figure 7.2. Web site evaluation.

From *Using Pop Culture to Teach Information Literacy: Methods to Engage a New Generation* by Linda D. Behen.
Westport, CT: Libraries Unlimited. Copyright © 2006.

Web Tips and Tricks

Demonstrate Web tips and tools so that they continue to learn that there are always different and multiple ways to accomplish the same thing but that sometimes there are more efficient methods. Take them to a Web site and ask them how to save paper when printing the page. If they don't respond with different methods, demonstrate how to print highlighted selections, e-mail pages, links, or print from the printer-friendly option. Tell them that they will be saving trees and little bunnies that live under the trees. In addition, show them how to go back three pages with a single click from the browser toolbar, or how to locate a word or phrase in a lengthy document by doing a word search in "find on this page." Allow students to offer more tips, and you might learn something new to teach to another class. Again, it's not necessarily the specific tips and tricks that are essential to students, but the fact that students are engaged in locating and accessing information while using your search methods and tips. Teens need to be reminded that there are always more efficient ways to navigate the Web and that no one will ever know everything there is to know about it (or about anything else for that matter).

Music, Audio, and Video Tools

Students love media, and they are great learning tools for those who are more visually and audio oriented. Students often tell us that they really do focus better when listening to music. Who are we to doubt it? You might want to provide headphones in the library for students or teachers who drop in to the library to listen to music or audio clips and for viewing videos that stream from the Web or that are on CDs or DVDs. Embrace all the bells and whistles that engage students, and teach them to locate and use them on their own at home or in your library. Remind them and their teachers that many educational media are available for classroom use and some include items that they already own, such as iPods. Ask students if they know they can use an iPod to record an interview or a class discussion, listen to audio books, and save documents and images. Almost daily, there are new and exciting educational tools available through the Web. Most are free, and you don't have to be a techie to learn about them, but you do have to be observant and perhaps a bit tuned in to technology through newsletters, journals, listserves, or people with whom you interact daily.

For instance, Google Earth, is one of Google's most recent innovations, and the basic product is completely free. It provides a three-dimensional look at planet Earth that flies users to any location in the world to zoom in on details such as cities, streets, schools, railways, parks, and hotels. You can travel with your students to Paris or Kenya for a geographic tour or get an aerial view of your school in your own city. Students and teachers should be able to find many educational purposes for Google Earth. Locate the product through Google (type Google Earth) and download the product to get started. In addition, the Public Broadcasting Service has a site dedicated to teachers and curriculum (http://www.pbs.org/teachersource/) and the National Public Radio (http://www.npr.org/) offers educational newscasts that can be used in the classroom. An extra bonus is that many of the videos and audio files are primary resources.

Again, it's not the single sites and programs that offer audio or video that you are selling to students, but the awareness and ability to locate effectively the endless formats offered for enjoyment and educational purpose. Students sometimes need permission and encouragement to use the newest tools that look and feel like toys. While instructing students about locating information on their topic, add a strategy or browse a database index that offers media and demonstrate the video, audio, and images associated with their topic. Remind them how powerful these resources may be for projects that include a class presentation or PowerPoint slide show. Don't forget to teach them (or have them demonstrate) how to import the media into their projects.

Ebooks

If ebooks haven't entered your library yet, they will soon. Ebooks are many things. They can be electronic versions of textbooks, audio books downloaded to an audio player, print downloaded to an ebook reader, or searchable online or downloaded nonfiction texts for research. More reference titles are being offered all the time, and the efficiency is obvious —students have access to ebooks 24/7, the searching component makes for quick and accurate searching (after you've taught them how to create search strategies), and they open up space on the shelves that you can reclaim for contemporary fiction and nonfiction.

Print books are here to stay, but ebooks are proving to be very useful as an addition. There's no need to remember which page the reference to Dolly Madison is found in a history reference book; you can just search for the term "Dolly Madison" and go to it immediately. Perhaps you aren't ready to go totally virtual with your reference collection, but your students are probably already using some ebooks from the subscription databases you have in the library. Make certain they know that they are using an ebook and that the information they are retrieving from the history or current topics database is copyrighted and possibly exists simultaneously in a print format. Help them make connections between print and electronic versions of books and articles to make certain that they understand how copyright, publishing, and use apply to all formats (see Publishing Basics). Everyone loves freebies, and students will want to know that there are free ebooks that they can use instead of buying all of the required reading books. They can also download many ebooks to a portable handheld device. Students will be excited to know that they can access and use entire books through the public domain (old enough to be out of copyright) that can be downloaded or printed or used to search tables of contents and chapters. Two large providers of public domain books are Project Gutenberg (http://www.gutenberg.org/) and the Electronic Text Center of the University of Virginia (http://etext.lib.virginia.edu/ebooks/).

In addition, Google Print and Amazon.com offer free limited searching of electronic books at their sites. Perhaps students will be frustrated by not being able to search more than a few pages of a book at these sites, but at least the Search Inside feature allows you, teachers, and students to locate useful books and make wise and informed purchasing decisions based on the table of contents and few pages of a book. Amazon.com also offers for sale thousands of electronic books to be immediately downloaded; there is no wait for your book to arrive through the mail, and there's no added shipping and handling fees. Many public library systems are adding ebooks that include new and popular titles to their collections; benefits include immediate access and increased circulation of ebooks among patrons due to the immediate return of items when the loan period expires.

No matter how you feel about ebooks, it's evident that they offer efficiency that print books can't, and they are becoming a common format for booksellers and libraries.

Communication Tools

Blogs, e-mail, and instant messaging can be both a blessing and pain for schools. We know that students communicate electronically instead of paying attention in class or working on schoolwork. And there's the added worry of using electronic tools for cheating. But what about the paper notes that get passed around the classroom and the creative methods of cheating in years past? Have the opportunities for cheating and communicating during class really increased? To safeguard against cheating and playing during class time, you can purchase remote control software for your networked computers that will allow the instructor to view students' desktops to make certain that they are on task. This type of software also allows the instructor or administrator to take control of the student's computer and to end sessions remotely or to demonstrate a task to a student without physically moving from her own desk. The advantages of new communication tools certainly outweigh the risks; at least e-mail and instant messaging communication can aid in classroom and group discussion about academic topics and projects or assignments and connect students to teachers and experts in a field. Promote e-mail, blogging, and instant messaging as additional resources for academic purposes and locating credible information. Talk openly about the advantages and disadvantages. You can also demonstrate the usefulness of the tools by sending announcements and electronic library newsletters to both students and teachers and setting up blogs or discussion groups through e-mail or chat rooms. The business office will thank you for using less paper and encouraging the use of efficient and economic resources.

RESEARCH SKILLS

Boolean Operators and Punctuation

Remind your students how they can't possibly know what term an author would use to describe something before they see the author's work. Remind them that research always involves some educated guessing and lots of trial and error. Students will be eager to learn the tips and tricks of searching when you approach them with a plan to save them time and trouble. The best information skills you can impart to them will translate to accessing the most valuable resources and enable them to easily use the skills in high school, college, and beyond. Ask your students to volunteer to demonstrate how they locate information on a topic. Give them credit for getting it started, and then show them how to do it more efficiently and accurately with resources that are obviously credible.

Use a current news topic to demonstrate how to create a sophisticated search strategy and explain the reason why they might need to broaden a term such as "Baghdad" to "Iraq" or "Middle East" to locate materials.

Here's an example: in a single search demonstration, show them how to locate information about teen life in Baghdad by using Boolean logic and search punctuation. Use the root word, teen*, with truncation punctuation and connect that to the broader term of "Iraq" with the Boolean operator AND. Tell students that in a single search, they are searching for teen, teens, teenager, and teenagers AND Iraq. The results should include all materials about Iraq and some form of teen. Broaden the search to include the Middle East by separating Iraq and Middle East with the Boolean operator OR to receive a broader selection of hits. Here is the search as it might appear in an electronic catalog (Figure 7.3):

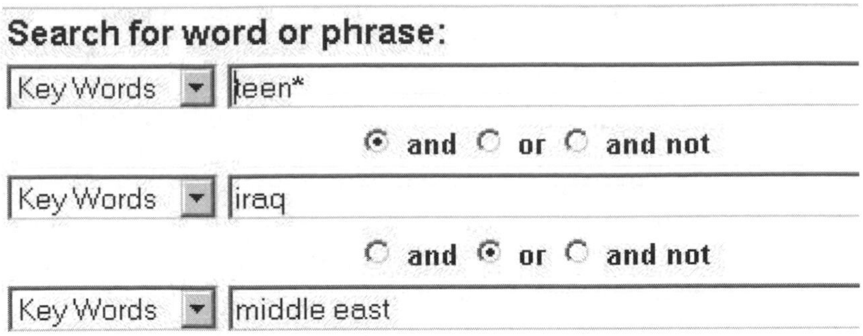

Search for word or phrase:

| Key Words ▼ | teen* |

◉ and ○ or ○ and not

| Key Words ▼ | iraq |

○ and ◉ or ○ and not

| Key Words ▼ | middle east |

**Figure 7.3. A possible search strategy for locating information about teens
in Baghdad using an electronic catalog.**

Ask if that seems less tedious than searching for each form of the word "teen" and each region, country, or city separately. Remind students to use the index and table of contents to locate more specific or related topics in a print book and explain why authors and publishers may be more likely to create books about teens in the Middle East rather than teens in Baghdad or Basrah. If necessary (if students still have trouble believing that they won't find exactly what they need), you can search for teen* AND Baghdad to demonstrate how many fewer results, if any, will be returned.

The same theory applies when students are searching for information about a single teen activity such as dating or education. The topic may be within a larger book or material but isn't the main or only focus of the item and won't be returned if searched for specifically.

Advanced Interfaces

Depending on the grade level, you can proceed with more complicated search strategies, or, for all grade levels, demonstrate the exact strategy in different resources so students can see the similar and differing results. You might want to suggest that students choose the advanced search interface in all databases, electronic catalogs, and search engines so that they are presented directly with the Boolean operators and indexes from which they can choose. Discuss why one might choose to search by keyword instead of subject and demonstrate the different results of both. Also, point out to students how they can choose specific date ranges and types of material.

Evaluating Results

Students expect that any matches to their search strategies will likely be the answer to their information needs, and they often start printing from the top of their result list to the bottom without much discrimination. Tell them that the result list is the beginning of their search for information. The search strategy is only the tool to get them to the results where they begin the evaluation process that will uncover the information they need.

Walk them through the basic steps of information evaluation before they even begin to read the content:

1. Does the title relate to your information need?

2. Who is the author or editor, and is she or he credible?

3. How current is the information, and is this relevant to your information need?

4. In what publication does the article appear? Is it an appropriate source?

After students determine that the titles satisfy these steps, they begin to evaluate the content of the information with four more steps:

1. Is the format and level of writing, vocabulary, introspection, and authority appropriate for my needs?

2. Does the article or book satisfy my information query or need?

3. Can I apply information from the article in my work or assignment?

4. What sources did this author use, and can I find related works?

Students are often impatient at this point and want to begin assimilating information into their assignment or work without carefully reading and evaluating of the materials. They need to learn to assess the information they gather before they proceed to make certain that the information satisfies their need and that they have enough to support their thesis or query. Students also quickly become personally involved with their topics and will relentlessly search to find exactly what they think they need. Perhaps it's because they've had so much information available to them since they were babies, but they are always amazed when they learn that there isn't a lot of research on their topic (that's age and level appropriate). Remind them that their ultimate goal in researching and completing an assignment is to learn the process that will serve them in other assignments and needs and to assimilate the information into a successful project that satisfies their academic goal. Some students need permission and confirmation from you that they should leave those topics (when permitted by their teacher) that prove very difficult to locate information about or to narrow or broaden the topic. Or, in many cases, students can apply the information found for a topic and use critical thinking skills to develop their own conclusion for a related topic. For example, if they can find a literary criticism about Fitzgerald's symbolic use of color in *The Great Gatsby*, they can then transfer that knowledge and symbolism to another Fitzgerald work. At that point, they will have moved from information gatherers to the knowledge and wisdom levels of information literacy.

Allow your students (at least upper-level students) the opportunity to search college or university and large public library electronic catalogs. Ask students where they hope and plan to go to college, and use one or more of those college electronic catalogs for the demonstration. Ask them to apply their skills and knowledge to this source. Tell them that experienced researchers (even library gods and goddesses) need to locate the common elements of a library electronic catalog and apply what we know to them. Remind them to look for ways to use Boolean operators and search punctuation and how to limit to specific formats or locations. If available, demonstrate how to place a hold on an item or have it sent to a specific branch or location of the library for easy pickup. Show students how they can access databases from a local college or public library, and demonstrate how to apply similar strategies to reap similar or different results.

The possibilities of information literacy are endless, and everyone determines what is essential for themselves and their students. As long as we continue to move students along the path toward information wisdom, we will be satisfying their need to become savvy and independent information users. Take a look at the "Checklist for the Essentials" in Figure 7.4 and use it or adapt it to your school's needs. Remember that the process is dynamic and will change almost constantly. Be flexible and make the instruction engaging and meaningful to your students.

Checklist for the Essentials

Technology and Media

❑ Your School's Network and Policies—Why and How

❑ Remote Access Usernames and Passwords—Why and How

❑ Information Sources—So Many Options

❑ Everybody and Anybody Can Create and Post a Web site

❑ Advertising and Web sites

❑ Web site Evaluation

❑ Web sites versus Proprietary Databases

❑ Citing and Bibliographies

❑ Web Tips and Tricks

❑ Music, Audio, and Video Tools

❑ Ebooks

❑ Communication Tools—E-mail, Blogs, Instant Messaging, and Chatting

Publishing Basics

❑ Publishing Facts

❑ Authors—Who are they?

❑ Print versus Electronic—delivery methods

❑ Copyright and Plagiarism

Research Skills

❑ Boolean Operators and Punctuation

❑ Basic and Advanced Search Interfaces

❑ Information Evaluation

❑ Other Library Electronic Catalogs and Databases

Figure 7.4. Are you covering the essentials?

From *Using Pop Culture to Teach Information Literacy: Methods to Engage a New Generation* by Linda D. Behen.
Westport, CT: Libraries Unlimited. Copyright © 2006.

Chapter 8

Build Your Information Literacy Instruction with Pop Culture

REALITY TV

I've been a huge *Survivor* fan since the first series aired on CBS in July 2000. I haven't missed a series and very few episodes. I even applied and sent in an audition tape in 2001. But my personal interest wasn't what motivated me to create the "Who Will Survive in the Library" PowerPoint presentation and challenge into my library instruction. The *Survivor* buzz was all over school. I'd hear students and teachers talking about Rudy, Richard, or Jenna, and I thought that it would be easy and fun to create a game from it.

When I sat down to create the presentation, the first version practically created itself. I looked at my Graded Course of Study (see Chapter 5) and made certain that I was covering all the standards I needed for the specific class (I later made different versions to adapt to different grade levels, subjects, and assignments). I created *Survivor* money and ten challenges to test students' knowledge of information literacy throughout the game. We set up a large, paper palm tree in the library for atmosphere and hung fish streamers from our ceiling. The display outside the library was also in theme. I bought American Library Association (ALA) "Read" bracelets and tattoos for grand prizes and our own library pencils for everyone else.

Before the first session, I talked with teachers about incorporating the game into their library class instruction. Although they looked at me like I was crazy, they all agreed and a few were even excited because they were *Survivor* fans as well.

Students entered the darkened library amid the palm tree and the projected "Who Will Survive in the Library" slide (see Figure 8.1). I asked them to wait to log on to computers until everyone was present, and then I had them count off into tribes of five or six students. They moved to sit near their tribe, logged on, and the game began.

I explained the rules and purpose of the game and tempted them with prizes to participate and earn *Survivor* money. Students' competitive nature took over by the second challenge, and hands popped up over the entire library to answer the challenge. I gave extra points for original answers or for suggestions that I hadn't mentioned. Occasionally I gave bonus points for being the first to answer or for very thoughtful and original responses. Some challenges required that students come up to demonstrate on the computer for points. They had to locate a book in our catalog and locate it on the shelves. I tried to appeal to all learning styles, and I asked each student how she located the answer instead of just what the answer was. Students were teaching each other with the different strategies and approaches.

Students participated beyond my highest expectations. But I knew that it would take some time to discover if the new style would pay off by increasing information literacy skills. Sure, they had fun and loved winning prizes, but I wondered whether I'd see and hear students remembering more about copyright, search strategies, and quality of information.

Some teachers formally tested students on the content. I love it when they take the instruction seriously and incorporate it into their curriculum. I thank them for doing so by giving them candy, bookmarks, or a public thank you in the electronic library newsletter that goes out to everyone at our school.

Students immediately became engaged with the *Survivor* Library Game, and I even received a CD of the *Survivor* soundtrack as a gift from some students that I added to my presentation. But after a year and a half, I was getting a little bored—even with different versions—and worried that students might be too, so I decided to add *The Amazing Race*, another reality TV show, to my presentation repertoire.

Eventually, I created versions of the different games for specific classes and assignments, and I still tweak the presentations constantly. For example, I look for and add other pop culture themes to keep students interested, or I change individual challenges (depending on the group) to inspire students to think critically. For higher-level classes, you assume that students already have some information literacy knowledge, and you might want to begin with challenges that will determine whether you need to review or move on with more sophisticated information. To involve students more quickly in a less intimidating way, I add bonus questions that are not knowledge based but that reinforce desirable behaviors. For example, I'll award five bonus points for students who have their library card or library card number with them.

We allow the game to flow with the energy of the specific class, but we do enforce one strict rule: all students must reply at some time during the game to ensure active participation by everyone. Collaboration among tribe members is encouraged to promote teamwork. I warn that points will be deducted from team's final score if some individuals don't participate. I've never needed to deduct points because it's rare that someone doesn't participate, and if I notice that an individual or two haven't spoken, I will remind the class that everyone must participate. The reminder has always been enough to encourage those individuals to respond at least once and to remind the more enthusiastic players to encourage their team members and to allow everyone to have a chance to play. Figures 8.1 and 8.2. show how we introduce the game and its rules.

Figures 8.3 and 8.4 are examples of how to keep the session focused on information literacy. The "U" in Figure 8.3 represents the first step in our school's research model that uses the acronym "URSULA."

Figures 8.5 and 8.6 are two examples of challenges that reinforce what you are teaching about information literacy.

Figure 8.1. *Survivor* introduction.

Figure 8.2. *Survivor* **rules.**

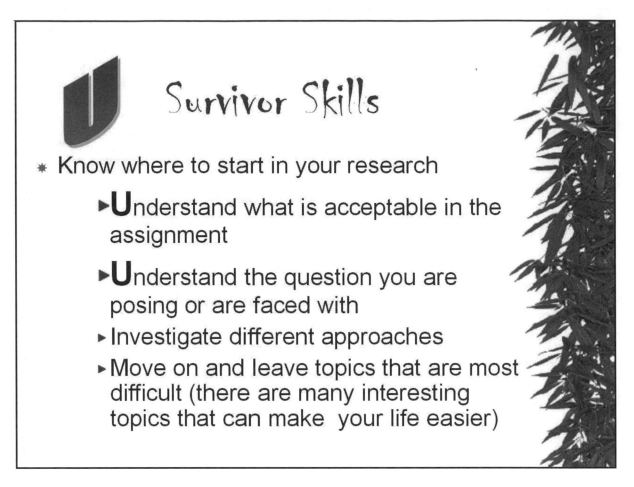

Figure 8.3. The first step in research involves an understanding of the assignment.

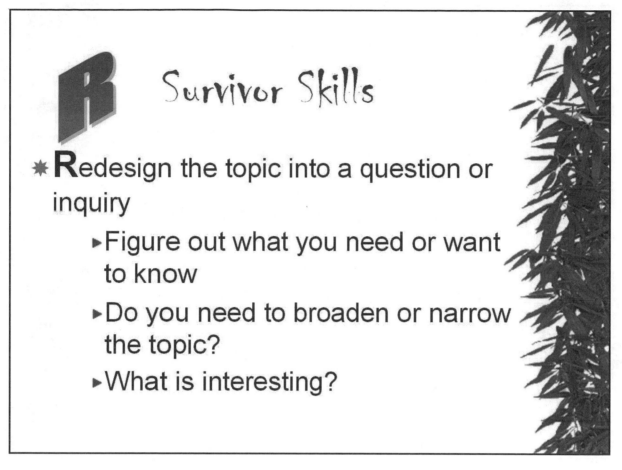

Figure 8.4. Students must create a relationship with their topic.

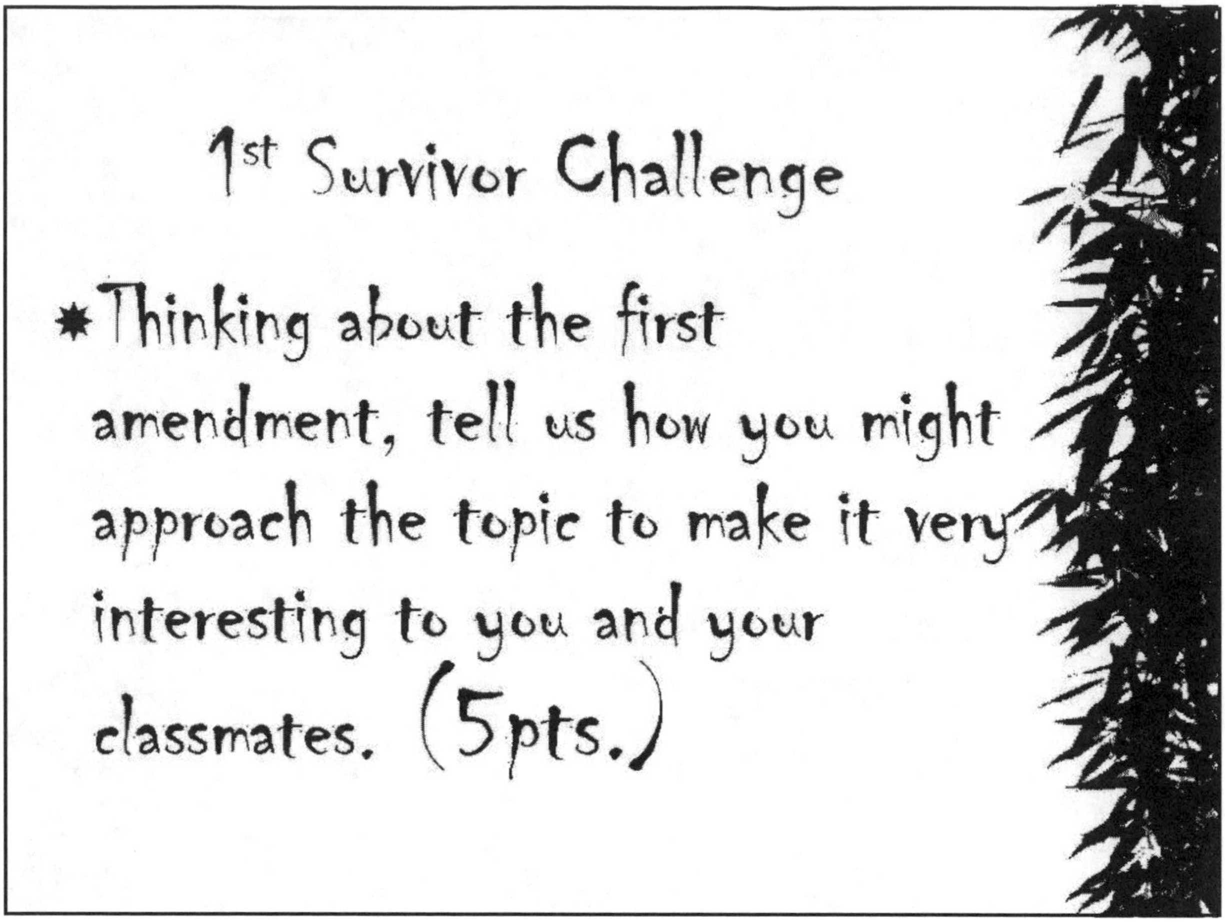

1st Survivor Challenge

* Thinking about the first amendment, tell us how you might approach the topic to make it very interesting to you and your classmates. (5pts.)

Figure 8.5. Challenge students to think beyond information gathering and fact finding.

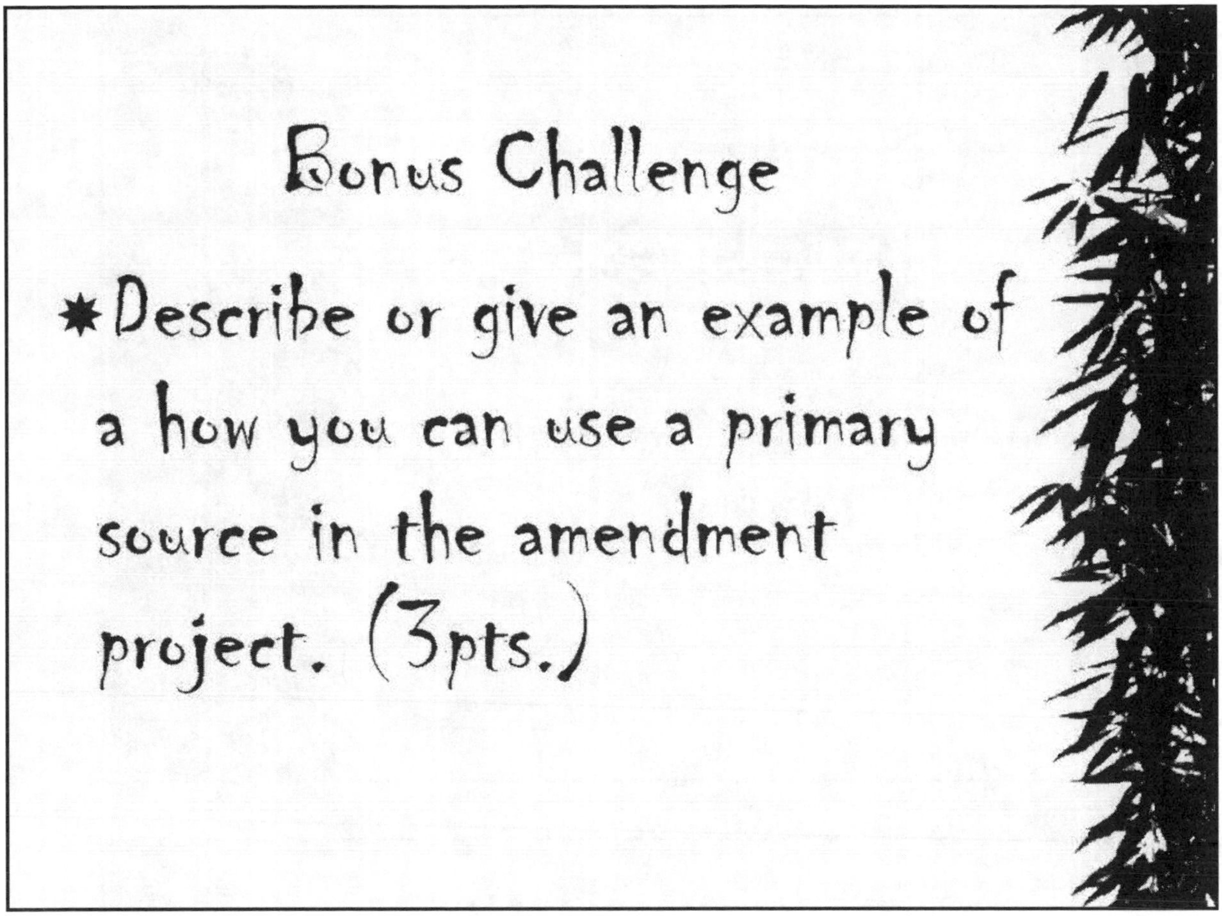

Figure 8.6. Allow students to demonstrate their critical thinking skills by applying important information literacy knowledge to a specific assignment or topic.

For a specific class assignment, adapt the *Survivor* Game to fit the research needs and the sophistication of the students. Figure 8.7 is an example of the complete presentation for an upper-level class. Notice the more advanced topics of information literacy.

The Amazing Race (Figures 8.8–8.13) is a more complicated game format and adds more twists and turns. Game cards that indicate Roadblocks, Detours, and Shortcuts are added features that keep the game constantly changing and interesting. I create and use laminated cards with diverse and interesting challenges that students select from a stack at appropriate times to keep the game interactive. Figures 8.8 through 8.11 are sample slides of challenges that students face in the game.

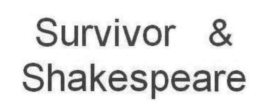

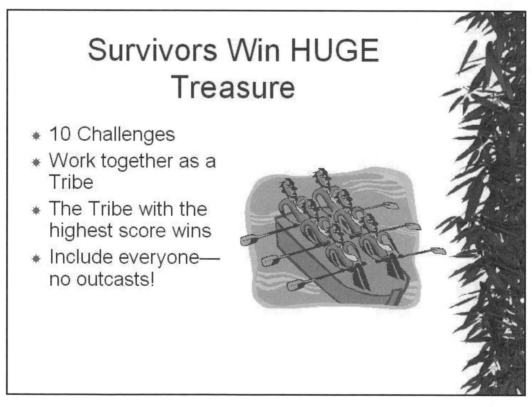

Figure 8.7. A *Survivor* game for juniors and seniors studying Shakespeare's *Merchant of Venice*.

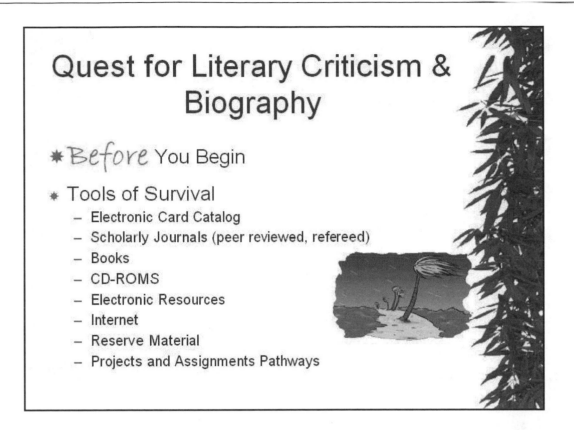

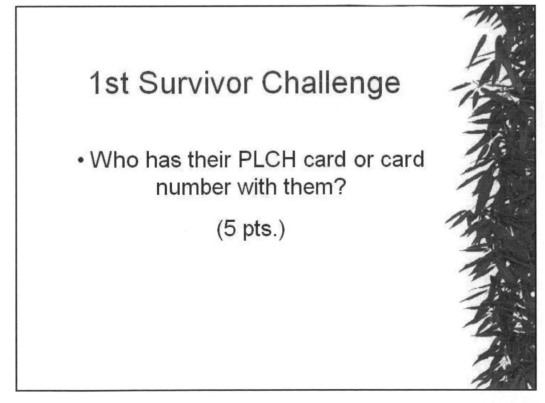

Figure 8.7. A *Survivor* game for juniors and seniors studying Shakespeare's *Merchant of Venice*.
(Continued)

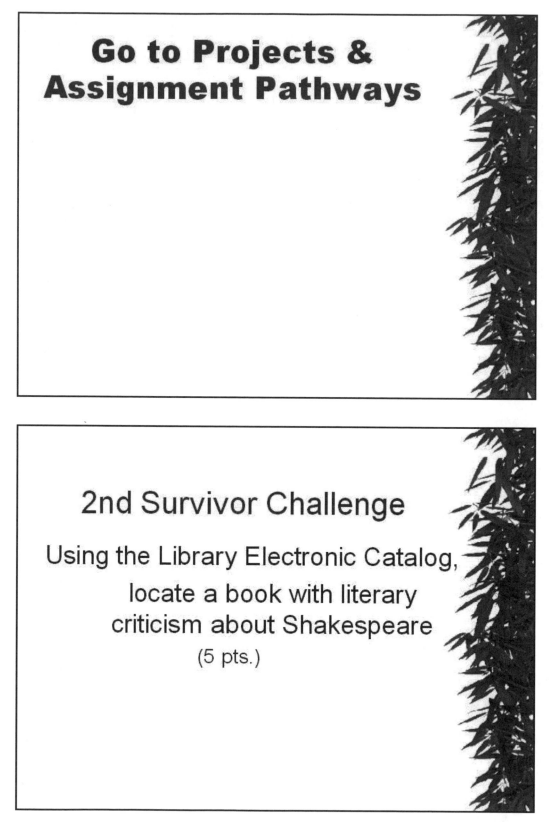

Figure 8.7. A *Survivor* game for juniors and seniors studying Shakespeare's *Merchant of Venice*. (Continued)

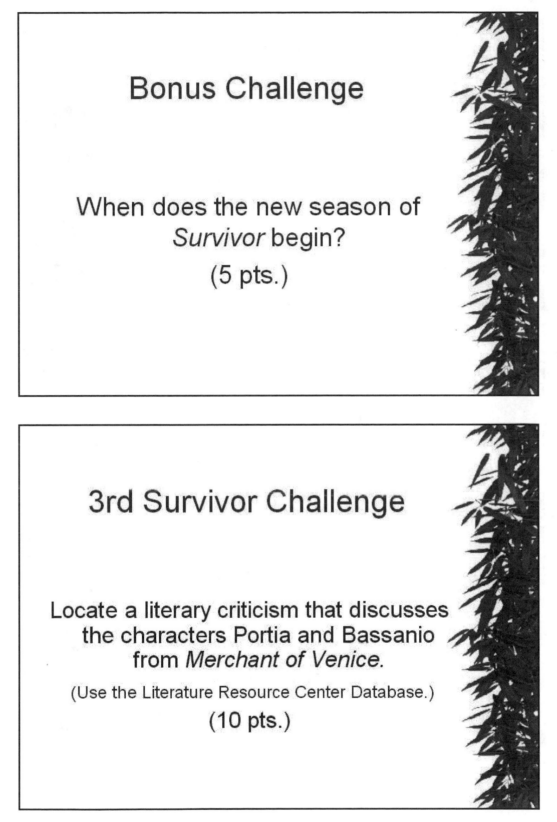

Figure 8.7. A *Survivor* game for juniors and seniors studying Shakespeare's *Merchant of Venice*. (*Continued*)

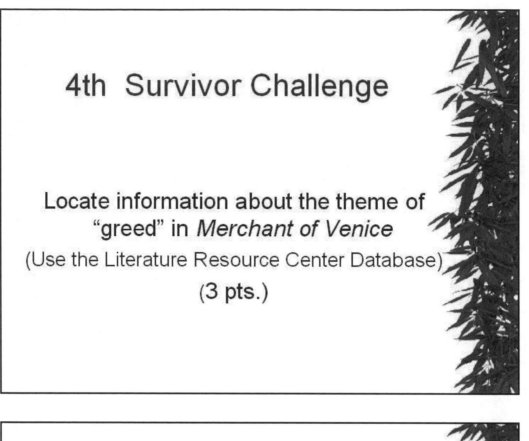

4th Survivor Challenge

Locate information about the theme of
"greed" in *Merchant of Venice*
(Use the Literature Resource Center Database)
(3 pts.)

5th Survivor Challenge

Using a Web site from the Projects &
Assignments pathway or from our catalog,
find information about the author of a critical
essay on the *Merchant of Venice.*
(10 pts.)

Figure 8.7. A *Survivor* game for juniors and seniors studying Shakespeare's *Merchant of Venice.*
(Continued)

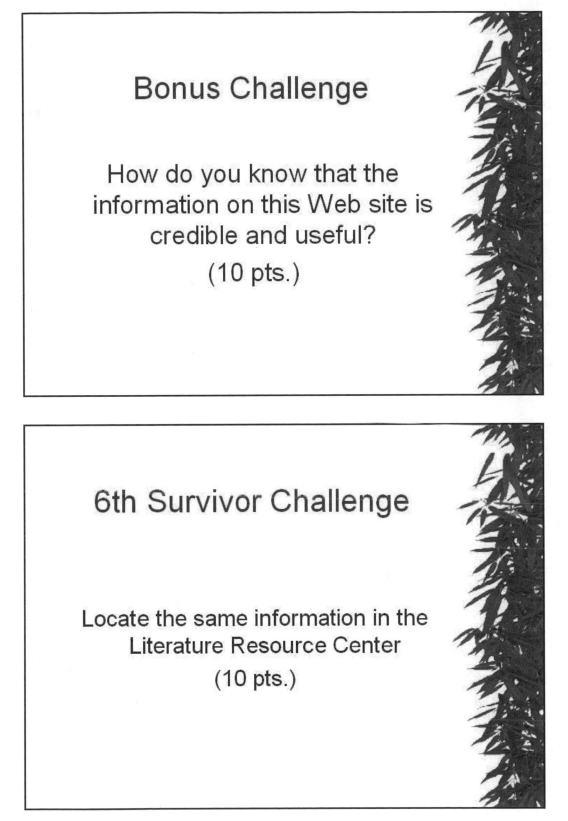

Figure 8.7. A *Survivor* game for juniors and seniors studying Shakespeare's *Merchant of Venice.*
(Continued)

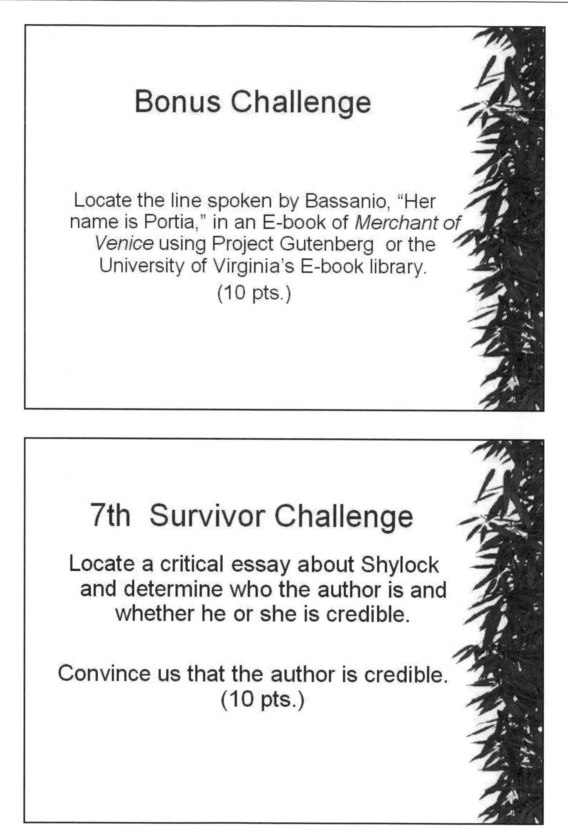

Figure 8.7. A *Survivor* game for juniors and seniors studying Shakespeare's *Merchant of Venice.* *(Continued)*

9th Survivor Challenge

Locate a book that involves the
character of Shylock in the
Merchant of Venice.
(You can search our library or another library)

(5 pts.)

10th Survivor Challenge

Locate a book in the PLCH catalog that
discusses the *Merchant of Venice* and the
theme of Shylock as a Jew.
(10 pts.)

For 5 more points, show us how to place a
hold on the item.

Figure 8.7. A *Survivor* game for juniors and seniors studying Shakespeare's *Merchant of Venice.*
(Continued)

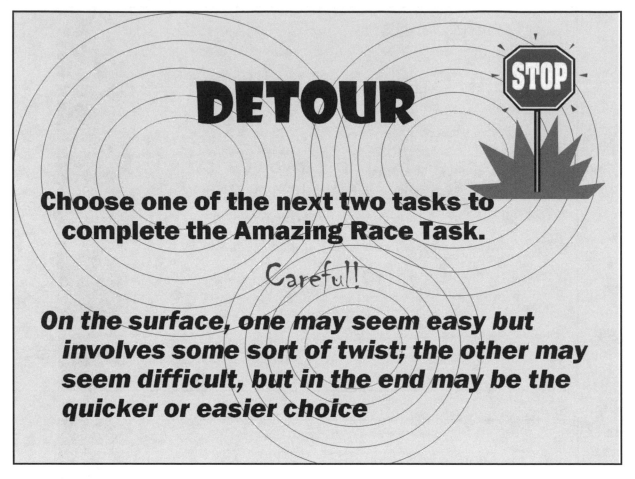

Figure 8.8. *The Amazing Race* Detour.

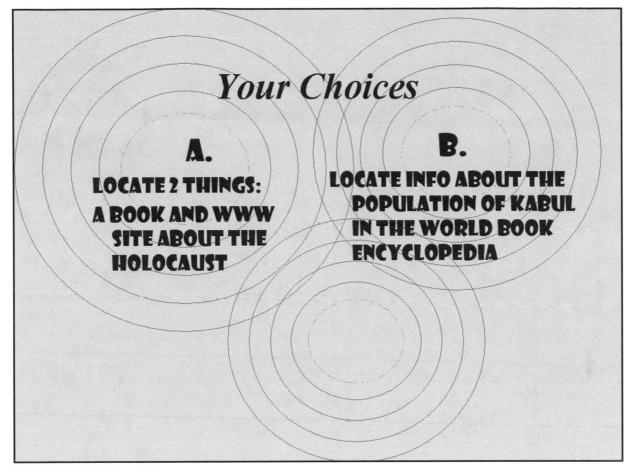

Figure 8.9. Two choices for *The Amazing Race* Detour.

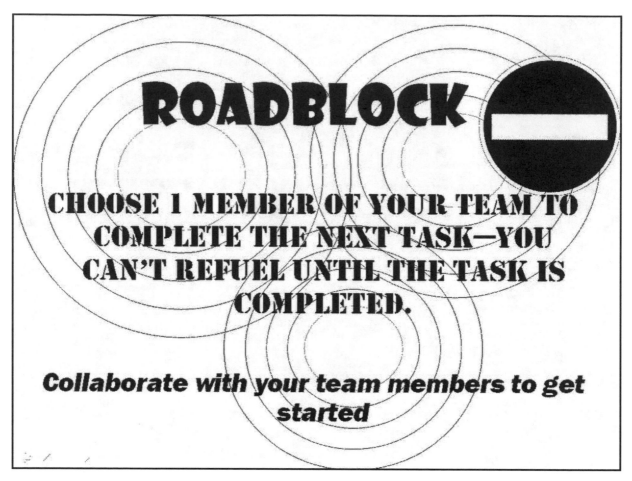

Figure 8.10. *The Amazing Race* Roadblock.

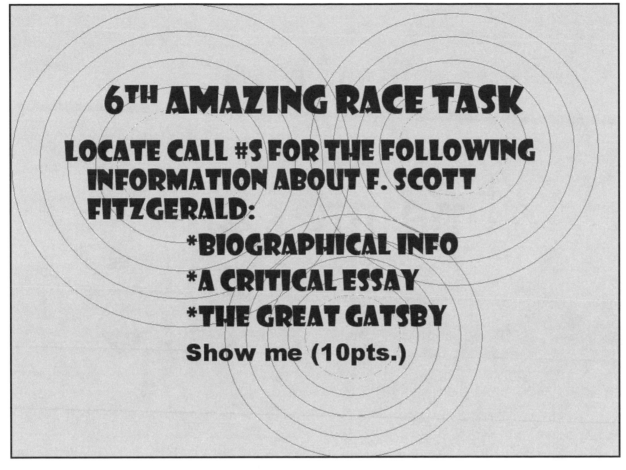

Figure 8.11. An *Amazing Race* Roadblock Challenge.

Figure 8.12. *The Amazing Race* Shortcut challenges.

SHORTCUT

3 points

Why would you choose to search
journals and magazines in a database
instead of paging through print issues?

Figure 8.13. A challenge for a freshman or sophomore class.

GAME SHOWS

Do you have classes in your school that don't have comprehensive testing at the end of the terms or teachers who prefer activities instead of exams? Offer them the option of coming to the library for an information game that tests their knowledge of both information literacy and class content in a fun and engaging way. Work with the teacher to develop the challenges from class topics and create the game specifically for that class and curriculum. You can use the template to create a game for different classes.

We've used *Who Wants to Be a Millionaire* (very loosely) to create "Who Wants to Be an Infoaire" for sophomore health classes. The game offers challenges on the topics covered during the term, and bonus questions are added to reinforce pleasure reading, current events, or critical thinking. Many challenges require students to demonstrate searching and locating information, and we encourage them to do most of the demonstrating and instructing during the game. Teachers can easily use the game and the results of the challenge as a final quiz by acting as scorekeeper during the game. Of course, students must be aware of how the game affects their grade before the game begins. Take a look at some sample slides (Figures 8.14–8.17).

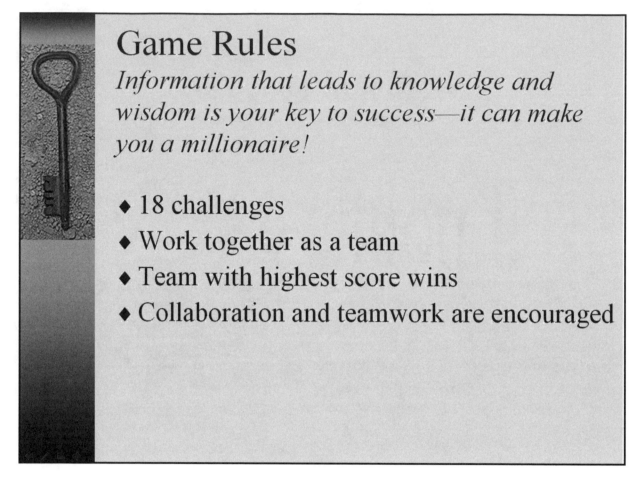

Figure 8.14. Game rules for "Who Wants to Be an Infoaire?"

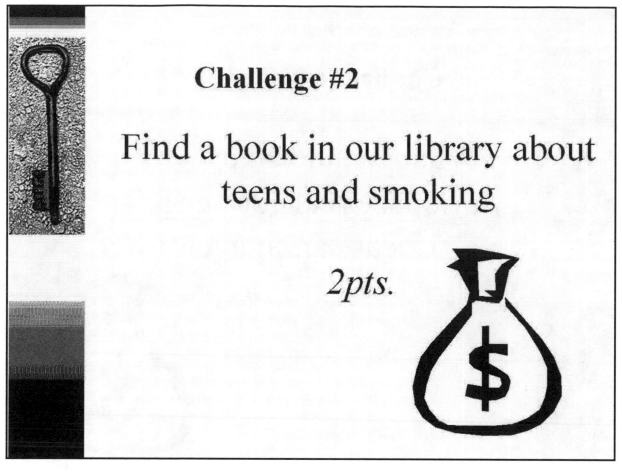

Figure 8.15. Topics from health class are used for these challenges.

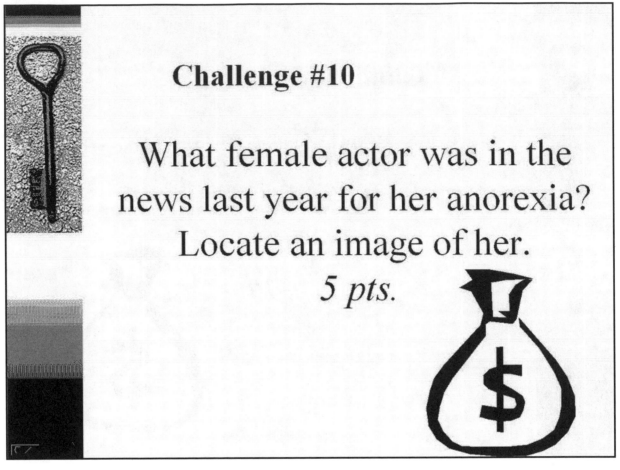

Figure 8.16. Add current news topics that are interesting to teens for bonus questions and to reinforce skills.

Challenge #13

Give us 4 reasons why making copies of the summer reading book for your friends might not be a good idea.

15 pts.

Figure 8.17. Bring discussions of plagiarism down to the students' level of interest.

MOVIES

It doesn't take a lot of effort to know what movies are hot with teens. Since the *Napoleon Dynamite* movie hit the theatres, we've seen "Vote for Pedro" T-shirts, costumes of the movie's characters at Halloween, and themed dances, and we've heard movie lines almost daily. We even had two music and dance acts performed in a recent faculty and staff talent show. The theme is a natural hit for any high school instruction. We made simple hand-written "Vote for Pedro" and "Vote for Summer" posters to hang in the library for atmosphere, and students broke up into teams that supported either the Summer or Pedro candidacy. You can also create new candidacy teams from the students themselves. Who wouldn't want to be the winner of the election in *Napoleon Dynamite*? Figures 8.18 and 8.19 offer a few ideas.

To make something tangible for students to hold during a game, create game money, points, or, in this case, votes to reflect the theme (Figure 8.20).

Figure 8.18. The movie *Napoleon Dynamite* gets students' attention.

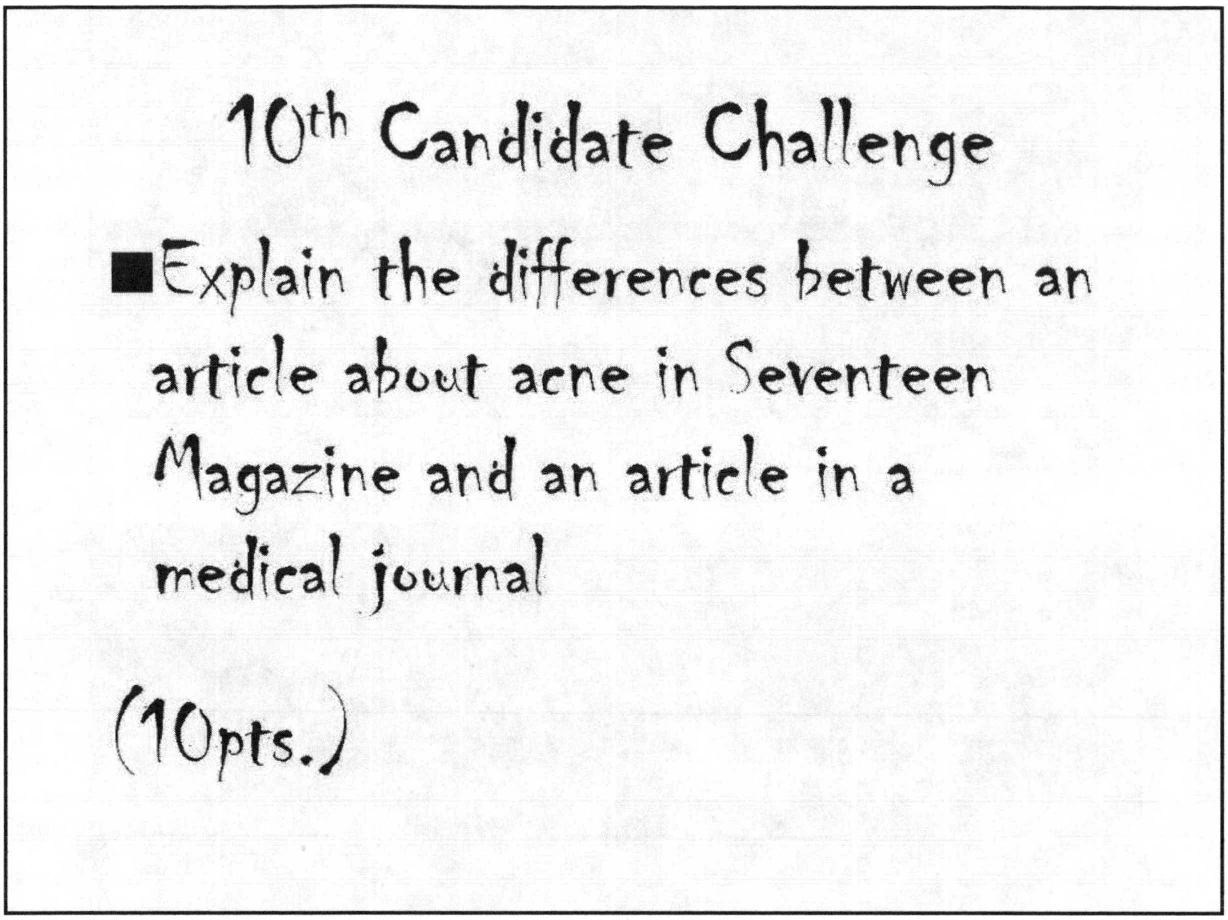

10th Candidate Challenge

■ Explain the differences between an article about acne in Seventeen Magazine and an article in a medical journal

(10pts.)

Figure 8.19. A typical challenge in the *Napoleon Dynamite* game that reinforces information literacy skills.

Figure 8.20. Details make the game more fun for students.

OTHER USEFUL TOOLS AND SAMPLES

Schoolwide Information Literacy Model

After attending many workshop and conference sessions about information literacy, studying the published standards, and reviewing and evaluating my own experiences at my school, we created the following research and information literacy model. I played with acronyms to find one that students would easily remember and that fits naturally into our program (Figure 8.21).

St. Ursula Information Literacy Steps

U	Understand the task—follow the teacher's guidelines
R	Redesign the topic into a question or inquiry—use critical thinking skills
S	Select the appropriate information resources—research, read, and understand
U	Understand the quality of the information—evaluate and analyze
L	Launch the project—assimilate information into your assignment—use the information effectively to create a thesis and body of work
A	Assess the final process and project or assignment—determine how you did? Do you need to repeat any steps?

Figure 8.21. A research model example from St. Ursula Academy of Cincinnati. Any word can be adapted to become an acronym.

Almost any acronym can be applied by changing the research model verbs so that the first letters work together to create the acronym for your school. For example, you can create an acronym for your mascot. If your mascot is a bulldog, you might use the following method (Figure 8.22).

B	**B**egin with the teacher's guidelines and understand the task
U	**U**nderstand the information need and redesign the question into an inquiry
L	**L**ist and use the information resources that will be most helpful for this project. Research, read, and understand
L	**L**earn from the information you gather. Evaluate and analyze your information
D	**D**esign your project by creating a thesis and outline
O	**O**rganize and assimilate the information into your body of work
G	**G**auge the quality of your work, evaluate what you learned and what you created, and return to former steps if necessary

Figure 8.22. Adapt any word to develop an acronym.

Compare the "BULLDOG" example to the "URSULA" acronym and notice how easy it is to change verbs and terminology to suit your needs.

Project Pages

Many of you already create sites that bring together the most appropriate resources and sources for a specific assignment or project. Librarians have always created bibliographies, and this takes the idea a step further by including links to your library's electronic catalog, the best databases for a specific research project, the teacher's assignment page, Web sites that you or the teacher have determined to be useful, and perhaps a Web site evaluation form or citing formats. If the teacher has reserve materials, it's a perfect location to include them. Post the project page as a Web site so that students and parents have access 24/7. Ask the teacher for time to walk students through the page and individual resources (it's a good chance for review) and make certain that everyone is sent away with remote access usernames and passwords for all resources that require them. The following examples (Figures 8.23 and 8.24) show the project and assignment Web pages and links to the sources that students will need for chemistry and classics projects. You can offer descriptions of Web pages or databases on the secondary pages along with the specific links to each source. And even offer suggested search strategies or search terms to remind students how to best search for the information they need.

Saint Ursula Academy Library

We Are Family
Chemistry Term 2 Project

Teachers: Ms. Wainscott and Ms. Hansen

Assignment	Library Catalog	Citing and Bibliographies
WWW Sites	Electronic Resources	WWW Site Evaluation Form

Figure 8.23. Sample chemistry project page.

Roman Emperors

Teacher: Mrs. Wilkey

Assignment

Library Catalog	WWW Sites	Citing and Bibliographies
Suggested Books	Electronic Resources	WWW Evaluation

Figure 8.24. Sample Roman emperors project page.

Parents' Night in the Library

Students are not the only patrons and stakeholders in our schools. Building relationships with teachers and staff is of obvious importance, but what isn't so obvious is the importance of connecting with your students' parents. Parents are valuable stakeholders for both the library and the school, and it never hurts to give the library and yourself a little positive publicity. Provide special events just for them. For example, send e-mail, print flyers, and announcements in newsletters or other publications inviting them to attend a Parents' Night in the Library. Busy parents often lag behind their children in technology skills and are very eager to get help using computers, software, and information resources. An informal and educational social event will allow new parents a chance to take a closer look at their child's learning environment and to interact with one or more of their educators. If the session has space for more participants, invite teachers and staff to ensure a good mix of participants. Parents will take away much more than technology and research skills after interacting with you and other teachers.

If you hold your session in the early evening, many parents will be arriving directly from work without dinner. Provide light refreshments and give each parent a folder with a handout of the PowerPoint presentation, a pencil, paper, and a copy of your usernames and passwords sheet. Ask for research topics of interest or have several that will interest them; topics that should interest parents are travel, health, or parenting. Cover the information sources in your library and their public library, demonstrate simple search strategies, and discuss how to determine good and credible information. And, perhaps most important, inform them about what you teach their children about information literacy. Create a short PowerPoint presentation to begin the event and help to focus participants. Have fun with the event, interact with your parents and let your skills and interest in information literacy impress them. Figures 8.25 through 8.27 offer a few ideas.

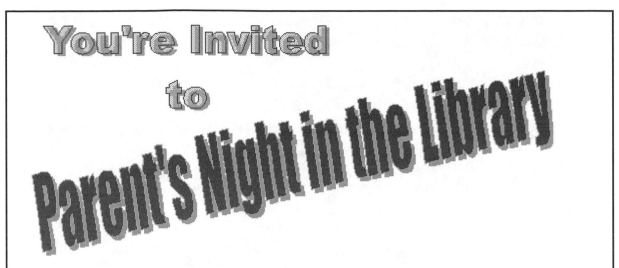

Spend 90 minutes in our St. Ursula's Academy library learning the tips and tricks to research.

> ➤ Learn how to find information about health, parenting, travel, etc.

> ➤ Find out what resources your child uses at school and how you can access them from home.

> ➤ Do you know that your daughter has access to materials from almost any library in Southern Ohio and Northern Kentucky because she's a St. Ursula student? Find out how.

When: Thursday, September 8, 2005, from 5:00–6:30 pm

Where: St. Ursula's Library

Who: Linda Behen, Director of Library Services

How: contact us at lbehen@saintursula.org or our school phone # x124 to reserve a seat (limit 30).

Figure 8.25. Parents' Night in the Library invitation.

Become a Savvy Library User in 90 minutes

Linda Behen
Director of Library Services
St. Ursula Academy

What's a Savvy Library User?

- Knows what the library has to offer
- Knows where to locate needed information
- Locates information quickly and easily
- Discerns between useful and worthless information
- Never goes "informationless" due to lack of skill or knowledge

Figures 8.26 and 8.27. A brief, formal presentation will help to focus your audience for the evening.

Chapter 9

Publicizing the Ultimate Library Program

Who is responsible for making certain that all students, teachers, and administration understand the importance of the library media center and information literacy? It's a chicken-and-egg question, and rather than focus energy and time in answering the question, jump in and make certain that you do everything possible to broadcast the ultimate library program that you've created. Don't risk someone not knowing what you offer to students, teachers, administrators and parents. Be bold in publicizing yourself and the library as the most valuable resource in school. Demonstrate your information expertise by solving your teachers' and administrators' information needs quickly and thoroughly and by teaching students the methods, skills, and tricks to locating information themselves as a result of your library program curriculum or any teachers' request. Most important, don't turn anyone away without providing the needed information; at the very least, make contact with someone who can provide it.

RESEARCH PROVIDES EVIDENCE

We all know what we do is valuable and how our library program affects our students' learning. We also know that many don't understand what we do or how we enrich their students' lives. Current professional research supports our value as librarians and media specialists and demonstrates that students succeed and are more information literate when robust library programs are present in their schools. For instance, the Research Foundation paper "School Libraries Work!" (Scholastic Library Publishing, 2004) compiles findings and results from almost a decade of studies that cite the measurable impact of school libraries and library media specialists. Cited is a 2004 Ohio study, "Students Learning through Ohio School Libraries" (Todd & Kuhlthau, 2004) that demonstrates how effective librarians and media specialists are as educational partners in articulating information literacy standards. Some of our libraries are in states that have a history of recognizing and rewarding libraries and library programs (although it's a constant struggle to hold on to that support), but we still have a tough time getting meaningful time with students and recognition for our valuable programs in our own buildings. So how do we shout above the daily noise of the education wheel to make teachers and administrators hear and understand us and to allow us to become the hub of that wheel?

There are many ways to distribute information about the importance of library programs, and it may be as simple as sharing or quoting the supporting statistics and results as often as possible and to provide the published research about libraries. Fourteen states and their research findings are included in "School Libraries Work!" and, as the publication states, "14 states can't be wrong." If your library is in Alaska, Colorado, Florida, Iowa, Massachusetts, Michigan, Minnesota, Missouri, New Mexico, North Carolina, Ohio, Oregon, Pennsylvania, or Texas, you have a document with evidence from your state's department of education to give to those who need to know. If your library is in another state, the documents and the related research from those states might be just what you need to arouse the interest of your administration and teachers. Beyond wanting to make the world a better place through information literacy, job security is a most legitimate reason to incorporate the best information literacy program into your school. Boldly demonstrate and broadcast your importance in your school or district.

BROADCAST YOUR LIBRARY PROGRAM

If you feel that you've spread the good word as much as possible and that unbelievers or the uninitiated still remain, simply do the work of a dynamic library program and put all those services and your information literacy instruction into action making certain that everyone knows about what you can do for them and their students. Take credit for the hard work and innovations that you've brought to your school; this is no place to be modest. Developing information-literate students is a goal far too important to risk not having the students, teachers, and administrators understand and support every means to achieve that end. Take a look at the following ideas for broadcasting your program and keeping it in the spotlight.

Create a Library Handbook

Create a handbook for teachers and administrators that compares the highlights of your program to standards. Highlight the services you provide that help to meet those standards. Update the handbook annually. Be certain to make it visually attractive so that students, parents, and teachers want to pick it up and read it. If you don't have the technology or graphic arts skills to pull off the project, ask students to help you. Choose to have them teach you, or have them do the work. Be sure to give them recognition and let them team with you for other publications. They get something to add to their portfolio, and you get a great looking publication.

Send a Multimedia Message

Create a DVD or video of what you do and show or distribute it at the beginning of the year to parents, students, new teachers, administrators, and even teachers who don't take advantage of what you offer. Offer to present your video at the first in-service of the school year, or post it on the Web so that everyone begins the school year with the same information about the library. Include portions of your interaction with classes, a demonstration of how to search the library catalog, and an orientation to library rules, services, and resources. Not only will it inform in a visual and entertaining way, but it also demonstrates how technology can be used innovatively. Recruit students to help produce the DVD. Let them play the leading role as narrator and present the library from a student's perspective. If you have a production studio, a multimedia lab, or a technology club in your school, the students can do all the technical preparation and production, and you can focus on the content and your role as producer and director. Make certain that it stays up-to-date and that a new version is ready when needed.

Use an Electronic Newsletter

Send monthly electronic newsletters (Figures 9.1 and 9.2) to offer the most recently acquired materials, describe or offer library contests and programs, highlight important resources, link to professional development opportunities, provide technology tips and tricks, offer help with lesson plans and technology. Include a Material Request form. I recommend electronic versions instead of print because they can be created more quickly, they have the ability to link to sites, and they use no paper unless individuals print them out on their own printers (using their own ink or toner and paper). In addition, they are easily saved, deleted (banish the thought), and they demonstrate an appropriate and efficient use of technology. Send a student version of your newsletter that informs students of the most recently acquired books, contests, announcements, and links to student-orientated Web sites.

Library Newsletter
January 2005

NEH Summer Seminars and Institutes for Teachers	Used Book Sale	Project pages and library instruction	
Christmas Break Reading Contest	Material Request Form	Faculty and Staff Resource Collection Ideas?	Teen Poetry Slam April 25, 2005 at Raymond Walters. Want to get involved? Let me know: lbehen@saintursula.org

Figure 9.1. An electronic library newsletter is an efficient way to broadcast your library's services and materials.

Student Library Newsletter

October 2005　　　　　　Library Hours
　　　　　　　　　　　　　　7:30 am – 5 pm

Freshmen—We want to meet you! Come see us in the library!

New stuff in the SUA Library *Fiction* *Nonfiction*	Online Homework Help 24hrs./live chat	Online Book Club from the Public Library of Cincinnati & Hamilton County	Public Library's Library Card Challenge *Coming in September!*
News	*Help with Citing* *Be wary of any info on the Web and make sure that it is exactly what you MLA books states.*	*Digital Cameras in the library*	*Give us the word* *Let us know what services or materials you want in our library*

Figure 9.2. The student version of an electronic library newsletter is
adapted for students' interests and needs.

Include a student version of the Materials Request Form (Figure 9.3) to invite students to offer suggestions for new titles and ask for students to submit book reviews that you publish in the student newsletter. We began our graphic novels collection as a result of the Materials Request form and graphic novel book reviews, and the collection has caused our circulation statistics to soar.

Library Material Request Form

Title: _____

Author: _____

ISBN #: _____

I don't know of a specific title, but I'd like items about _____

_____

_____

_____

Format: CD-ROM, Print Book, Magazine, Software, ETC. (please circle or fill in other format)

_____

I'd like to be contacted as soon as item arrives _____Yes _____Not necessary

Other comments or suggestions:

**Figure 9.3. A Material Request Form for both students and faculty can
be valuable in collection development.**

From *Using Pop Culture to Teach Information Literacy: Methods to Engage a New Generation* by Linda D. Behen.
Westport, CT: Libraries Unlimited. Copyright © 2006.

Submit a State of the Library Report

Provide self-generated State of the Library Reports for your principal and administrators. A quarterly or annual summary of library services, activities, circulation and collection development statistics, participation in professional development, participation in professional organizations, grant proposals written and grants awarded, new programs and report of participation, for example, will no doubt pleasantly surprise administration with all that you do, and it can also be used as a justification for budget requests.

Become a School Leader

Become a school leader by participating in every appropriate decision-making committee or council that exists in your school. Without representation in decision-making bodies, the library is easily forgotten and opportunities are lost. Become one of the individuals in your school whom the administration can depend on to be visionary, organized, and dependable. Offer workshops and technology aid to teachers, students, parents, and administration. Don't hide your knowledge under a book cart. The more expertise and knowledge you share, the more confidence the stakeholders at your school will have in your skills, abilities, and judgment.

Connect with Your Students

Stay connected with your students. With all the planning, scheduling, program creation, acquisition tasks, material processing, committee work, and budget balancing that goes on behind the scenes in a school library, it's easy to become the person behind the curtain that students never see. Don't let that happen. Put your face in front of students as regularly as possible. Trade places during the day with your assistant at the circulation desk or volunteer to moderate student clubs, service programs, and other activities that will let you interact with students. There is no better way to stay in touch with their world and to become approachable to students than direct interaction.

Connect with Parents

Stay connected with parents. Parents can provide support and volunteer aid for day-to-day operations and educational issues and needs. Provide special programs for parents so that they can see how libraries have changed since they were students and how they can reinforce at home what your instruction is teaching their children at school. Invite them for an afternoon or evening of library or technology instruction. Let them experience technology tools that can save time. Give them your usernames and passwords so they, too, can use your databases and help their children. Recruit library volunteers to help with book fairs, used book sales, collection maintenance, or special projects. Their help not only benefits your daily operations but also brings fresh ideas and attention to the library.

Be Award Winning

Apply for local, regional, or national awards for your innovative programs and collaborations with teachers that work. Nominate yourself or ask a trusted teacher or colleague to nominate you. Even if you don't personally care about awards, your administrators do because if you look good, they look good—and ultimately, the school looks good. Also, it's a great way to get recognition and attention for what you need teachers in your school to know and the ways you hope to collaborate with them.

Go for the Grants

Write grant proposals that result in money for your library and school. Money speaks very loudly, and it quickly gains administrators' attention. More important, with all the money available for creating innovative technology in schools and libraries, it will provide you with the means to try new things. For example, we acquired a multimedia lab for video creation and editing through a LSTA (Library Services and Technology Act), and as a result, students come to the library regularly to design, create, and edit astonishingly creative and complicated videos for class assignments and projects. In fact, the acquisition of the lab has created a demand that now requires us to seek additional funding for expansion.

If the idea of writing grants sends shivers through your body, you're not alone. As with everything else, taking it one step at a time will make it manageable. Talk to others in your school district or your library network that have written grants successfully and have them walk you through the steps involved. Most funding organizations make it fairly simple by requiring very specific steps and guidelines to follow and many grant-awarding organizations offer workshops or sample proposals to review. Your first proposal might seem overwhelming, but when you receive that letter of congratulations and the money for your project, you will quickly forget the steps and time it took to create the proposal. As a final word of caution, make certain that you have a couple of trusted colleagues review your proposal for typos and clarity before sending it off. If they have questions, chances are the review team will, too. Most grants are very competitive, and you don't want to lose out because of missed typos or ambiguity.

Become a Technology Expert

Help teachers integrate technology into their curriculum. Become the expert (either formally as part of your job description or informally) that teachers ask about new gadgets and technology and who they rely on for ideas. A simple way to share in lesson plan development is to create project and assignment Web pages where students can locate the best resources and links for a specific project (see Chapter 8). Easing the teachers' workload by providing credible and reliable resources will bring those teachers back to you and your library program for assistance time and time again. Word spreads quickly among departments and teachers, and it won't take long for you to become the person to provide things for them. Offer to walk their classes through the project and assignment pages to remind students about differences among the library catalog, literary databases, and Web pages. The captive audience of students permits the opportunity for you to review or teach topics of information literacy.

Standardize Your School's Research and Information Literacy Efforts

Finally, as stated in earlier chapters, a method that is rapidly becoming standard for many schools and school libraries is the research and information literacy model. There are many existing research models that attempt to make research and information literacy manageable and simple for students. In researching various models (see Chapter 5), you'll find that all research models break down an information need into categories of understanding the information need, locating and accessing information, evaluating information, and assimilating it. Establishing a model is probably the single best method to ensure that all stakeholders in your school have the same expectations with regard to writing, research, and information literacy. It takes a commitment to consistency and reinforcement in every department and by every educator with every project and assignment to produce information-literate students.

REFERENCES

Scholastic Library Publishing. (2004). "School Libraries Work!" Retrieved January 2, 2005, from http://www.scholasticlibrary.com

Todd, Ross J., Kuhlthau, Carol C., & OELMA. (2004). "Students Learning through Ohio School Libraries" [online]. Retrieved December 10, 2004, from http://www.oelma.org/studentlearning/default.asp

Index

About the Author

LINDA D. BEHEN is the Library Director at St. Ursula Academy, Cincinnati, Ohio. She has received numerous grants and awards to enhance her library service, and has been a reviewer for several library journals including *Catholic Library World* and *The Book Report*.